The ſlaues are ours, So do I anſwer you.
The pound of fleſh which I demand of him
Is deerely bought, 'tis mine, and I will haue it.
If you deny me; fie vpon your Law,
There is no force in the decrees of Venice;
I ſtand for iudgement, anſwer, Shall I haue it?

Du. Vpon my power I may diſmiſſe this Court,
Vnleſſe *Bellario* a learned Doctor,
Whom I haue ſent for to determine this,
Come heere to day.

Sal. My Lord, heere ſtayes without
A Meſſenger with Letters from the Doctor,
New come from Padua.

Du. Bring vs the Letters, Call the Meſſengers.

Baſſ. Good cheere *Anthonio.* What man, corage yet:
The Iew ſhall haue my fleſh, blood, bones, and all,
Ere thou ſhalt looſe for me one drop of blood.

Ant. I am a tainted Weather of the flocke,
Meeteſt for death, the weakeſt kinde of fruite
Drops earlieſt to the ground, and ſo let me;
You cannot better be employ'd *Baſſanio,*
Then to liue ſtill, and write mine Epitaph.

Enter Nerriſſa.

Du. Came you from Padua from *Bellario?*

Ner. From both.
My Lord *Bellario* greets your Grace.

u whet thy knife ſo earneſtly?
feiture from that bankrout there.
ale : but on thy ſoule harſh Iew
keene : but no mettall can,
Axe beare halfe the keenneſſe
an no prayers pierce thee?
thou haſt wit enough to make.
an'd, inexecrable dogge,
ice be accus'd:
wauer in my faith;
Pythagoras,
infuſe themſelues
n. Thy curriſh ſpirit
o hang'd for humane ſlaughter,
s did his fell ſoule fleet;
in thy vnhallowed dam,
For thy deſires
ſteru'd, and rauenous.
raile the ſcale from off my bond
Lungs to ſpeake ſo loud:
outh, or it will fall
nd heere for Law.
Bellario doth commend
octor in our Court;

heere hard by
To know your anſwer, whether you'l admit him.

Du. With all my heart, Some three or four of you
Go giue him curteous conduct to this place,
Meane time the Court ſhall heare *Bellarioes* Letter.

*Y*Our Grace ſhall vnderſtand, that at the receite of your
Letter I am very ſicke : but in the inſtant that your meſſenger came, in louing viſitation, was with me a young Doctor of *Rome,* his name is *Balthaſar:* I acquainted him with
the cauſe in Controuerſie, betweene the Iew and *Anthonio*
the Merchant : We turn'd o're many Bookes together: hee is
furniſhed with my opinion, which bettered with his owne learning, the greatneſſe whereof I cannot enough commend, comes

with him at my importunity, to fill vp your Graces requeſt in
my ſted. I beſeech you, let his lacke of yeares be no impedime nt
to let him lacke a reuerend eſtimation : for I neuer knewe ſo
yong a body, with ſo old a head. I leaue him to your gracious
acceptance, whoſe trial ſhall better publiſh his commendation.

Enter Portia for Balthazar.

Duke. You heare the learn'd *Bellario* what he writes,
And heere (I take it) is the Doctor come.
Giue me your hand : Come you from old *Bellario?*

Por. I did my Lord.

Du. You are welcome : take your place;
Are you acquainted with the difference
That holds this preſent queſtion in the Court.

Por. I am enformed throughly of the cauſe.
Which is the Merchant heere? and which the Iew?

Du. *Anthonio* and old *Shylocke,* both ſtand forth.

Por. Is your name *Shylocke?*

Iew. *Shylocke* is my name.

Por. Of a ſtrange nature is the ſute you follow,
Yet in ſuch rule, that the Venetian Law
Cannot impugne you as you do proceed.
You ſtand within his danger, do you not?

Ant. I, ſo he ſayes.

Por. Do you confeſſe the bond?

Ant. I do.

Por. Then muſt the Iew be mercifull.

Iew. On what compulſion muſt I? Tell me that.

Por. The quality of mercy is not ſtrain'd,
It droppeth as the gentle raine from heauen
Vpon the place beneath. It is twice bleſt,
It bleſſeth him that giues, and him that takes,
'Tis mightieſt in the mightieſt, it becomes
The throned Monarch better then his Crowne.
His Scepter ſhewes the force of temporall power,
The attribute to awe and Maieſtie,
Wherein doth ſit the dread and feare of Kings :
But mercy is aboue this ſceptred ſway,
It is enthroned in the hearts of Kings,
It is an attribute to God himſelfe;
And earthly power doth then ſhew likeſt Gods
When mercie ſeaſons Iuſtice. Therefore Iew,
Though Iuſtice be thy plea, conſider this,
That in the courſe of Iuſtice, none of vs
Should ſee ſaluation : we do pray for mercie,
And that ſame prayer, doth teach vs all to render
The deeds of mercie. I haue ſpoke thus much
To mittigate the iuſtice of thy plea :
Which if thou follow, this ſtrict courſe of Venice
Muſt needes giue ſentence 'gainſt the Merchant there.

Shy. My deeds vpon my head, I craue the Law,
The penaltie and forfeite of my bond.

Por. Is he not able to diſcharge the money?

Baſ. Yes, heere I tender it for him in the Court,
Yea, twice the ſumme, if that will not ſuffice,
I will be bound to pay it ten times ore,
On forfeit of my hands, my head, my heart :
If this will not ſuffice, it muſt appeare
That malice beares downe truth. And I beſeech you
Wreſt once the Law to your authority.
To do a great right, do a little wrong,
And curbe this cruell diuell of his will.

Por. It muſt not be, there is no power in Venice
Can alter a decree eſtabliſhed :
'Twill be recorded for a Preſident,

And

LAW versus EQUITY in

The Merchant of Venice

Mr. WILLIAM SHAKESPEARES

COMEDIES, HISTORIES, & TRAGEDIES.

Published according to the True Originall Copies.

Martin Droeshout sculpsit London.

LONDON

Printed by Isaac Iaggard, and Ed. Blount. 1623.

Portrait of William Shakespeare from the title page of the First Folio, 1623.

LAW versus EQUITY

IN

The Merchant of Venice

A Legalization of Act IV, Scene I
With Foreword, Judicial Precedents,
and Notes

by MARK EDWIN ANDREWS

UNIVERSITY OF COLORADO PRESS

Boulder, Colorado

This book is dedicated to the memory of Professor J. Duncan
Spaeth of the Department of English of Princeton University,
who inspired it, and to Professor Roy M. Mersky of the School
of Law of the University of Colorado, who resurrected the manuscript from the Law Library archives after almost thirty years.

. . . Legal history has its true significance as the record of the unceasing struggle by which man has won his way from savage individualism to an organic society founded on the recognition of rights and obligations. The processes by which, through the centuries, they have been defined and individual liberty has been protected and reconciled with obligation—whether this has been done well or ill—and the procedures by which the legal doctrine of one epoch has been adapted to the next and made to serve the interests of a changing civilization, are the great lessons that legal history has to teach. We shall miss these lessons if we look upon the documents as dry and sterile parchments, of interest only because of their rarity, and fail to trace in them the vibrant pattern of the never-ending quest for justice, which is the noblest pursuit of man.

—HARLAN FISKE STONE

Preface

One spring day in 1964 John Moller, a librarian at the University of Colorado Law Library, was dutifully sorting a stack of dusty reports that had been stuffed untidily into a dog-eared pasteboard carton. These reports, which had accumulated for several decades, had titles too imposing to allow them to be discarded. Then one report caught Mr. Moller's attention. It was a sheaf of legal size bond, slightly yellowed with age and entitled *Law Versus Equity in 'The Merchant of Venice'*, written by a Mark Edwin Andrews in 1935.

Since Portia and Shylock are as much at home in legal circles as in English literature classrooms, Mr. Moller spent the evening reading this fascinating and well documented manuscript. It argued succinctly two points: first that Shakespeare displayed surprising knowledge of English jurisprudence and the English judicial system; and second that the system, in its attempt to straighten out the conflict between the common law and the principles of equity, was influenced by the bard's knowledge.

When the work was brought to his attention, Roy Mersky, head law librarian, recognized its merits and began a search for Mark Edwin Andrews. With the aid of *Who's Who* and a Houston telephone directory, the search was short. An exchange of letters followed and Mr. Mersky received the author's permission to publish the work.

Mr. Andrews, a law student when he wrote the manuscript, was inspired and encouraged in the project by the Shakespearean scholar, Professor J. Duncan Spaeth, with whom he was studying at the time. During the thirty years between the writing and "discovery" of his work, Mr. Andrews has been a law instructor, an industrialist, and for three years served as Assistant Secretary of the Navy.

Dr. Spaeth's admiration of the work was seconded by Justice Harlan F. Stone. After examining the manuscript in 1937, Justice Stone wrote the author:

"Often, in listening to *The Merchant of Venice,* it has occurred to me that Shakespeare knew the essentials of the contemporary conflict between law and equity. But until I read your manuscript I had never realized how completely the play harmonized with recognized court procedure of the time.

"You have done an admirable piece of work. . . ."

—J. K. EMERY, *Editor*

Foreword

The trial scene of *The Merchant of Venice*, in essence, is a treatise on the attributes and qualities of mercy. Now, as then, it provides a universal moral lesson, not only for the never-ending procession of Shakespeare's followers but also for all mankind.

Actually, if the play is studied in context with sixteenth century English jurisprudence, it becomes evident that Shakespeare was offering more than a sermon on the virtues of mercy. He was holding up a mirror for all to see the dramatic climax of an age-old conflict between the common law courts which dispensed unmitigated "justice" by the strict letter of the law, and the courts of chancery where "mercy seasons justice" to do equity.

In 1300, English common law was rigid and restricted. In contrast, the guiding principles of equity were beginning to emerge—flexible and free.

In about 1330, King Edward III, in spite of the objections of the common law judges, decided to allow his Chancellor to hear cases which the judges would not hear. The move had a dual purpose—to increase the King's revenue and to aid his subjects.

Thus sprang up two separate and different systems of jurisprudence. The common law courts acted *in rem* on the property of the litigants; the equity courts acted *in personam* on the person of the litigants. A conflict soon arose between these courts, and there followed a struggle which lasted approximately three hundred years.

About 1350, it became the common practice for one litigant, "Mr. A," to go into a court of common law and get a judgment against "Mr. B." Then "Mr. B" would go to the Court of Chancery and ask the Chancellor for help, possibly arguing that "Mr. A's" judgment was too harsh, or would do irreparable harm, or that the case was incorrectly decided. Sometimes the suit was on a bond such as Shylocke's; sometimes it was an action of debt, detinue, covenant, or account.

The Chancellor, after hearing the "cause in controversy," might issue a decree in favor of "Mr. B," if he thought "Mr. A's" judgment was inequitable for any reason. In his decree the Chancellor would not seek to overrule or nullify "Mr. A's" judgment. He would merely tell "Mr. A" that he would be put in jail indefinitely for contempt of the Chancellor's decree, if he tried to enforce his common law judgment on the bond, or on the debt, covenant, etc.

By the reign of Elizabeth (1558–1603), literally hundreds of cases were recorded in which one litigant had a *judgment* in his favor and the other litigant had a *decree* in his favor, in the same controversy.

In 1597, when the conflict was at its height, William Shakespeare, at 33, was a popular and successful playwright in London and a man of some substance. Francis Bacon, at the age of 36, had just published his *Essays* and was a leading lawyer of the day. Edward Coke, then only 45, was the

Attorney General and was soon to become Judge of the Court of Common Pleas. Thomas Egerton, who became Lord Ellesmere, was 56, was already Lord Keeper of the Great Seal, and was soon to become Lord Chancellor of the Court of Chancery. All of these men were living in or near London at the time. Coke, Ellesmere, and Bacon were members of the Inns of Court; and Bacon was a leading member of Gray's Inn when *The Comedy of Errors*, by William Shakespeare, was presented there. All were busily engaged in their own activities and the affairs of Queen Elizabeth's Court and the exciting life of London.

This is probably the year in which Shakespeare wrote *The Merchant of Venice*, dramatizing this struggle between law and equity. In the trial scene of the play, equity is victorious. Shylocke received a valid judgment on the "bond" Antonio had "signed" and "sealed" before a "notary"; but, because of the "decree" of the Chancellor, he could not enforce his "judgment" without spending the rest of his life in jail, or even losing his life under a strict interpretation of an existing statute pertaining to an alien who threatened the life of a citizen.

In 1615, a somewhat similar case (Glanvill vs. Courtney) arose on a bond. Lord Chief Justice Coke entered a judgment for the plaintiff. Lord Ellesmere, the Lord Chancellor, issued an injunction by a decree, thus preventing the enforcement of the judgment on the bond. King James I appointed Sir Francis Bacon to head a commission to advise the King, once and for all time to come, as to whether or not the Chancellor had the power to enjoin the enforcement of a common law judgment. Bacon advised the King that the Chancellor

had this power. Thus, Shakespeare, aware Elizabethan that he was, not only dramatized the struggle but also accurately predicted the victory for equity.

The author can advance no irrefutable proof as to the influence of the play on Elizabethan thought, or on the final decision regarding the case of Glanvill vs. Courtney. But is it not significant that Coke, Ellesmere, and Bacon saw each other frequently and must have had many opportunities to see the play, to discuss it with others who had seen it, and to discuss it among themselves? It is even possible that one or more of them may have known Shakespeare personally. That Ellesmere and Bacon were familiar with the play is quite clearly shown by echoes from the lines of the trial scene in their writings. (See Part II, note 10, page 27.)

To deny the existence and effect of such reciprocal influence is to assume that Shakespeare was oblivious to the most significant and dramatic conflict then shaking the foundations of English law when he wrote the trial scene, and also to assume that the "Imaginative Portrayal of Life in Shakespeare's Plays" had no repercussions among his audiences and no significance in terms of contemporary movements. The more that recent Shakespearean scholarship has helped us to understand the conditions under which he worked, the less likely such an assumption becomes.

To say that the predicament in which Shylocke found himself (he could have his pound of flesh but dared not take it) and the predicament in which Glanvill found himself in the case tried a few years later (he could exercise his rights according to a judgment at law but dared not because of the injunction) have nothing in common and are not "hewn from the same rock and digged from the same hole of the pit" is equivalent to saying that George Bernard Shaw was not mindful of the evils of prostitution when he wrote *Mrs. Warren's Profession* and the art of the distiller when he wrote *Major Barbara*.

Since the literary "Precedents" for the bond plot and the trial scene which were available to Shakespeare are considered in Part II, it is only necessary to state here that none of the recognized sources of the bond plot in *The Merchant of Venice* contains the strict adherence to legal forms and procedure, that none has the reference to contemporary legal problems and existing statutes, and that none makes use of the equitable devices found in the trial scene. (See Part II, note 1, pages 19 and 20.)

The attempt to produce a harmonious whole has determined the general plan of this work.

I shall sketch the source of the conflict between law and equity with bold strokes, but I hope I shall give sufficient details to bring out the fact that law and equity sprang from separate sources, that they attempted to solve judicial problems by different means, that there was an increasing rivalry between the two, and that the stage was set by an awakening of national consciousness. It was this sense of the greatness and glory of England which stimulated the national mind not only in the fields of adventure, colonial conquest, and expansion but which stirred creative activities in the field of law, as well as literature, and which stamps "the spacious times of great Elizabeth" as a period of fresh and spontaneous endeavor.

Part I consists of the exegetic proof of Shakespeare's knowledge of the difference between law and equity and of his accurate use of the terms of each. This is accomplished by a legal prose translation of three hundred and ninety-seven lines of the majestic poetry of the trial scene. The actual poetry of Shakespeare, taken from the Globe text, appears on the side margin of the page and is designated by lower case letters.

Part II makes available to the reader actual contemporary or prior cases to illustrate the legal and equitable points involved, placing before him the "opinions" of the best-qualified contemporary jurists, as well as expressions by outstanding legal scholars and historians on the development of the common law courts and courts of equity from the twelfth to the seventeenth century. The points raised in Part I are designated by footnote numbers referring the reader to the proper section of Part II.

When the trial scene is read with legal and equitable principles in mind, it divides into four parts.

The first part begins with the first words of the Duke: "What, is Antonio here?" (line 1). It ends with the Duke's statement: "Upon my power I may dismiss this court,/ Unless Bellario, a learned doctor,/ Whom I have sent for to determine this,/ Come here to-day." (104–106).

The second part, which is the admission of Portia, as *Amicus Curiae* (friend of the court), begins with the Duke's words to Nerissa: "Come you from Padua, from Bellario?" (119). It ends with the final common law judgment *in rem* which Portia prepares for the court: "A pound of that same merchant's flesh is thine:/ The court awards it, and the law doth give it." (299–300)

Prior to this part of the trial scene, the

terms used, the procedure, and the law applied have all been a part of the common law of the Court of King's Bench, of Elizabethan England when the play was written.

The third part begins when Portia says: "Tarry a little; there is something else./ This bond doth give thee here no jot of blood;/ The words expressly are 'a pound of flesh:'." (305–307)

Part three ends with Portia's words: "Thou shalt have nothing but the forfeiture,/ To be so taken at thy peril, Jew." In this part, for the first time, the principles, the procedure, and the maxims of equity, in a Court of Chancery, are used exclusively.

The fourth part begins when Portia repeats her previous warning to Shylocke and says: "Tarry, Jew:/ The law hath yet another hold on you." (346–347) She then cites the statute by which Antonio becomes the plaintiff and Shylocke becomes the defendant in what is known as a cross action. This statute is as follows: "If it be proved against an alien/ That by direct or indirect attempts/ He seek the life of any citizen,/ The party 'gainst the which he doth contrive/ Shall seize one half his goods; the other half/ Comes to the privy coffer of the state;/ And the offender's life lies in the mercy/ Of the Duke only, 'gainst all other voice." Then Portia shows the Chancellor that the statute is applicable in the following words: "In which predicament, I say thou stand'st:/ For it appears, by manifest proceeding,/ That indirectly and directly too/ Thou hast contrived against the very life/ Of the defendant; and thou hast incurr'd/ The danger formerly by me rehears'd." (349–362)

In the fourth part Shakespeare uses all of the devices of equity and the Court of Chancery to have mercy season justice.

Shylocke is enjoined from enforcing his common law judgment for a pound of flesh.

One half of Shylocke's property is put in trust for Antonio's use and benefit during the life of Shylocke. Upon Shylocke's death this one half then goes to Lorenzo who has married Shylocke's daughter.

The other half of Shylocke's property is put in trust, with the court as trustee, for the use and benefit of Shylocke, for his own life. After his death this half then goes in fee simple to Jessica, Shylocke's daughter, and to Lorenzo, and their heirs.

This disposition of the property could only be accomplished in a court of equity, by the use of trusts which were not allowed in common law courts at that time.

The proceedings end when the Duke says: "He shall do this, or else I do recant/ The pardon that I late pronounced here." (391–392) Then Portia tells the clerk of the court to "draw a deed of gift" (394). Shylocke then says: "send the deed after me,/ And I will sign it." (396)

The Duke then concludes the hearing by issuing his final decree, *in personam*, when he tells Shylocke: "Get thee gone, but do it." (397)

Rosetti says:

"The only true motive for putting poetry into fresh language must be to endow a fresh nation, as far as possible, with one more possession of beauty. Poetry not being an exact science, literality of rendering is altogether secondary to this chief law. I say *literality*, not *fidelity*, which is not the same thing."

The author has not attempted to create "one more possession of beauty," nor could he if he chose and, therefore, has striven for *fidelity* more than beauty in this attempt to make legal prose from Elizabethan poetry.

My obligations to the scholars whose efforts have made this work possible have been acknowledged in the notes.

I wish to express my great appreciation to Dr. J. Duncan Spaeth, Murry Professor of English Literature, of Princeton University who presented the issue of "Mercy versus Justice" in such an inspiring manner that it suggested to the writer the possibility of the solution of the so-called legal quibble by the powers of the Chancellor in a court of equity. In addition, I wish to acknowledge my gratitude to Dr. Spaeth for reading the manuscript so carefully and for his many suggestions which were incorporated throughout the work.

I am obligated to Professor W. S. Holdsworth of Oxford University for his excellent work, *A History of English Law*, which was used as a general source and guide to the authorities.

To Professor William Arthur of the School of Law of the University of Colorado, I am indebted for his detailed outline of the disposal of Shylocke's property, according to the decree, under the intricate equitable devices of the sixteenth century.

I wish also to express my appreciation to Professor Robert Smith of Lehigh University, to Professor H. H. Hudson, Chairman of the Department of English of Princeton University, to Justice Rutledge of the Supreme Court of the United States, all of whom read the manuscript and offered valuable suggestions.

To Justice Stone of the Supreme Court of the United States, I wish to express my gratitude for his comments on the manuscript and for the use of his very appropriate words at the beginning of the book.

The School of Law of the University of Colorado, because of the scholarly and broad interests of Dean James Grafton Rogers, is the possessor of many of the earlier *Year Books* to which I have had access. Had it not been for this fine library—which contains hundreds of volumes of early English reports, as well as most of the extant works of Coke, Bracton, Dugdale, Gilbert, Rolle, Selden, Style, and other English jurists—and the skill, ingenuity, and patience of Mrs. Cicely Sherwood, the librarian, this work would never have been accomplished.

M.E.A.

September 22, 1935

Contents

Illustrations

The most excellent

Historie of the *Merchant* of *Venice*.

VVith the extreame crueltie of *Shylocke* the Iewe
towards the sayd Merchant, in cutting a iust pound
of his flesh: and the obtayning of *Portia*
by the choyse of three
chests.

As it hath beene diuers times acted by the Lord
Chamberlaine his Seruants.

Written by William Shakefpeare.

AT LONDON,
Printed by *I. R.* for Thomas Heyes,
and are to be fold in Paules Church-yard, at the
figne of the Greene Dragon.
1600.

Title page from the First Quarto edition of The Merchant of Venice, *1600.*

Part I

In majestic poetry unwithered by age, Shakespeare dramatized the centuries-old conflict between law and equity in English jurisprudence. With due humility, the author has placed simple legal prose beside the poetry on the following pages to illustrate this fact.

Court scene in the Doge's Palace, Venice.

ACT IV

SCENE I. *London.*[1]* *A Court of Law.*[2] A.D. *1597*[3] *of the reign of Elizabeth, the thirty-ninth year,* LORD CHIEF JUSTICE COKE[4] *sitting.*

The Court. Is the defendant in Shylocke vs. Antonio ready?[a]

Antonio. The defendant is ready,[5] your Honor.[b]

The Court. Before proceeding with this trial let me advise you that I shall be forced to apply the law without mercy, for the plaintiff will insist upon it.[c]

Antonio. I understand your position and if he insists on his rights at common law, there is no legal defense to his suit.[d]

The Court. Proceed with the trial. Call the plaintiff, Shylocke.[e]

Enter SHYLOCKE.

The Court. The court, Shylocke, is loath to believe that you intend to press this suit to a conclusion and exact the penalty of the bond—a pound of flesh—but doubts not that, having carried the matter thus far, it is your intention not only to release the "forfeiture" of the bond and thus show your mercy[f] but also to relinquish your claim for a part of the principal debt. Since you have engaged no counsel,[7] I shall rely upon my prerogative to advise you to withdraw[8] this most unreasonable suit.

Shylocke. You have read my petition,[9] your Honor. I have sworn to have the forfeit of my bond.[g] The law is on my side. I need no lawyer to tell you that, if you deny me my right, you will be setting such a precedent[10] in this great city of London, the center of trade and commerce of the world,[11] that merchants will cease to have confidence in your courts and your laws and will thereafter no longer venture their goods and cargoes here. The resulting stagnation of trade and commerce on the Thames will ultimately make of London but a deserted village.[h] You ask me why I prefer a pound of the defendant's flesh to three thousand ducats. "I'll not answer that": [42]† It is immaterial and irrelevant[12]

SCENE I. *Venice. A court of justice.*

[a]*Duke.* . . . is Antonio here?

[b]*Antonio.* Ready, so please your grace.

[c]*Duke.* I am sorry for thee: thou art come to answer/ A stony adversary, an inhuman wretch/ Uncapable of pity, void and empty/ From any dram of mercy.

[d]*Antonio.* I have heard/ Your grace hath ta'en great pains to qualify/ His rigorous course; but since he stands obdurate/ And that no *lawful* means can carry me/ Out of his envy's reach,[6] I do oppose/ My patience to his fury. . . .

[e]*Duke.* . . . call the Jew into the court.

[f]*Duke.* Shylocke, the world thinks, and I think so too,/ That thou but lead'st this fashion of thy malice/ To the last hour of act; and then 'tis thought/ Thou'lt show thy mercy and remorse more strange/ Than is thy strange apparent cruelty;/ And where thou now exact'st the penalty,/ Which is a pound of this poor merchant's flesh,/ Thou wilt not only loose the forfeiture,/ But, touch'd with human gentleness and love,/ Forgive a moiety of the principal. . . .

[g]*Shylocke.* I have possess'd your grace of what I purpose/And by our holy Sabbath have I sworn/ To have the due and forfeit of my bond:

[h]*Shylocke.* If you deny it, let the danger light/ Upon your charter and your city's freedom.

---

* All notes designated by number appear in Part II.

† The line numbering is that of the Globe text.

[3]

and no more admissible than would be the question, why I should pay ten thousand ducats to have my house freed of one rat. I do not know why some men fear a harmless cat nor do I care, but I do know that I do loathe Antonio there.[a],* Does that answer your question?

[Shylocke now takes the witness stand and is cross-examined with ostensible superficiality, but with genuine keenness, when he is asked, "Do all men kill the things they do not love?" (66), to which the witness, who has been touched, replies "Hates any man the thing he would not kill?" (67)]†

Antonio. I pray you let us not delay longer. You may as well bid time and tide stand still. Let me confess judgment[17] and allow the plaintiff to enforce his bond.[b]

Friend of Antonio. In settlement of the case we offer you six thousand ducats; that's twice your bond.[c]

Shylocke. I would not settle for thirty-six thousand ducats.[d]

The Court. It is fortunate for you that you are in a court of law, in an action on your bond, for if you used such language in Lord Ellesmere's Court of Chancery you would be told "He who seeks Equity must do

---

* It is to be remembered that this part of the proceeding is in the Court of King's Bench. Had this statement been made before the Court of Chancery,[13] one of its great maxims, "He who seeks Equity must do Equity," would have come into play. But courts of equity and courts of law were not united until the Judicature Act of 1873.[14] At this time there was being waged the titanic struggle between the law courts under the leadership of Lord Chief Justice Coke and the Court of Chancery under Lord Chancellor Ellesmere.[15] This battle of the centuries—not of a century, for it began about A.D. 1300—culminated in a victory for the Court of Chancery in 1616, when it was held, in the leading case of Glanvill vs. Courtney, that, if there was an irreconcilable difference of opinion between the Lord Chancellor and the Lord Chief Justice, the decree of the Court of Equity should prevail over a judgment at law.[16]

† A possible answer to Dr. Spaeth's question of the meaning of this line, a line he said he never could understand:
1. Upon cross examination Shylocke has admitted that he bears Antonio a "lodg'd hate."
2. Shylocke then says you cannot really hate a man unless you would kill him.
3. Therefore, Shylocke, who admits his hatred for Antonio, would kill him.
4. Thus is supplied the *mens rea*, or criminal intent, which is *the* essential element for the crime of murder. It also brought Shylocke within the purview of one of the many informer statutes (see page 13).

[a]*Shylocke.* You'll ask me, why I rather choose to have/ A weight of carrion flesh than to receive/ Three thousand ducats; I'll not answer that:/ But, say, it is my humour: is it answer'd?/ What if my house be troubled with a rat/ And I be pleas'd to give ten thousand ducats/ To have it ban'd? What, are you answer'd yet?/ Some men there are love not a gaping pig;/ Some that are mad if they behold a cat;/ And others, when the bagpipe sings i' the nose,/ Cannot contain their urine: for affection,/ Mistress of passion, sways it to the mood/ Of what it likes or loathes. Now, for your answer:/ As there is no firm reason to be render'd,/ Why he cannot abide a gaping pig;/ Why he, a harmless necessary cat; . . . / So can I give no reason, nor I will not,/ More than a lodg'd hate and a certain loathing/ I bear Antonio, that I follow thus/ A losing suit against him. Are you answer'd?

[b]*Antonio.* I pray you, think you question with the Jew:/ You may as well go stand upon the beach/ And bid the main flood bate his usual height;/ You may as well use question with the wolf/ Why he hath made the ewe bleat for the lamb;/ You may as well forbid the mountain pines/ To wag their high tops and to make no noise,/When they are fretten with the gusts of heaven;/ You may as well do any thing most hard,/ As seek to soften that—than which what's harder?—/His Jewish heart: Therefore, I do beseech you,/ Make no more offers, use no farther means,/ But with all brief and plain conveniency/ Let me have judgement and the Jew his will.

[c]*Bassanio.* For thy three thousand ducats here is six.

[d]*Shylocke.* If every ducat in six thousand ducats/ Were in six parts and every part a ducat,/ I would not draw them; I would have my bond.

Equity,"[a, 18] "He who comes into Equity must come with clean hands," and that new maxim the Chancellor has just put forward that "Equity abhors a forfeiture"[19] or some such similar term.

Shylocke. I'm not in a court of equity, but a law court. "What judgement shall I dread," [89] I have done no wrong at law.[b] I have paid dearly for that which I demand. If you deny it, I am done with your law. I do not think there is any binding force to an equitable decree. I am relying on this court to give me a judgment at law, "shall I have it?"[c] [103]

The Court. The court will reserve decision[20] of this case until I have heard a lawyer from Cambridge, whom I have called as *Amicus Curiae*[21] in this case and whom I expect here today. This lawyer is Sir Francis Bacon,[22] with whom I do not always agree but for whose legal ability I have the most profound respect.[d] This is a novel case, involving a very important legal problem. I desire to have the points thoroughly briefed and argued before reaching a conclusion. I do not want either of the parties to this suit to be able to sue out a bill[23] in a court of equity and obtain there a decree which the Exchequer Chamber[24] might affirm.

Clerk of the Court. Your Honor, there is a messenger outside with a letter from the lawyer from Cambridge.[e]

The Court. Bring us the letters! Call the messenger!

Enter LAW CLERK.[f]

The Court. Are you from Cambridge—from Bacon?[g]

Law Clerk. I am from Cambridge, your Honor, and I bring you the respects and a letter from my lord, Sir Francis Bacon.[h]

Friend of Antonio. [Walking up to Shylocke, threateningly] You "inexecrable dog!" [128] It's creatures like you that lend credence to the theory that humans are the reincarnation of animals.[i]

Shylocke. You can't harm me with all your railing

[a]*Duke.* How shalt thou hope for mercy, rendering none?

[b]*Shylocke.* What judgement shall I dread, doing no wrong?

[c]*Shylocke.* The pound of flesh, which I demand of him,/ Is dearly bought;/ 'tis mine and I will have it./ If you deny me, fie upon your law!/ There is no force in the decrees of Venice.*/ I stand for judgement: answer; shall I have it?

[d]*Duke.* Upon my power I may dismiss this court,/ Unless Bellario, a learned doctor,/ Whom I have sent for to determine this,/ Come here to-day.

[e]*Salerio.* My lord, here stays without a messenger with letters from the doctor,/ new come from Padua.

[f]*Enter* NERISSA [dressed like a lawyer's clerk].

[g]*Duke.* Came you from Padua, from Bellario?

[h]*Nerissa.* From both, my lord. Bellario greets your grace [presenting letter].

[i]*Gratiano.* O, be thou damn'd, inexecrable dog!/ And for thy life let justice be accus'd./ Thou almost mak'st me waver in my faith/ To hold opinion with Pythagoras, / That souls of animals infuse themselves/ Into the trunks of men: thy currish spirit/ Govern'd a wolf, who, hang'd for human slaughter,/ Even from the gallows did his fell soul fleet,/ And, whilst thou lay'st in thy unhallow'd dam,/ Infus'd itself in thee; for thy desires/ Are wolvish, bloody, starv'd, and ravenous.

---

* If Shakespeare did not intend to make a distinction between the meaning of *decree* and *judgment,* as used herein, the one can be substituted for the other. When this is done the lines become meaningless, as shown by the following altered quotation:

> There is no force in the *judgements* of Venice.
> I stand for *judgement:* answer; shall I have it?

and curses; I'm used to them. Until you can talk the seal off that bond,[25] what you say accomplishes nothing.[a] I know that no contract or bond is enforceable in England unless there is a valuable *quid pro quo* or consideration contained therein. But so long as that seal is on the bond, it comes under the one great exception to that rule; for the seal itself, because of the solemnity of the transaction, has been held in this very court to be sufficient consideration to support such a contract. Ha! You see we vile money lenders are not stupid; we know the law and all the tricks you gentiles have so carefully taught us. What do you think I was doing when I made Antonio go before a notary[26] of the crown and execute and seal that bond?[b] I'll tell you; I was having him execute an instrument which I knew would be enforceable in this very court of law[27] and about which there could be no dispute,[28] so that I would not need a lawyer. I stand for law.

The Court. This letter from Bacon recommends a learned young lawyer to the court. Where is he?[c]

Law Clerk. He awaits your permission to practice before this court for he has never been admitted[29] here.[d]

The Court. I will admit him. Present him to the court. Let me hear the letter.[e] Bacon was the *Amicus Curiae* for whom I sent. If he commends his learning,[f] this young lawyer must be as quick and sharp as the thrust of a spear.

[The Court then reads the following letter from Sir Francis Bacon:]

"Your grace shall understand, that at the receipt of your letter I am very sick: but in the instant that your messenger came, in loving visitation was with me a young doctor of Rome; his name is Balthasar. I acquainted him with the cause in controversy between the Jew and Antonio the merchant: we turned o'er many books together: he is furnished with my opinion; which, bettered with his own learning, the greatness whereof I cannot enough commend, comes with him, at my importunity, to fill up your grace's request in my stead. I beseech you, let his lack of years be no impediment to let him lack a reverend estimation; for I never knew so young a body with so old a head. I leave him to your

[a]*Shylocke.* Till thou canst rail the seal from off my bond,/ Thou but offend'st thy lungs to speak so loud:/ Repair thy wit, good youth, or it will fall/ To cureless ruin. I stand here for law.

[b]*Shylocke.* Go with me to a notary, seal me there/ Your single bond. . . .

[c]*Duke.* This letter from Bellario doth commend/ A young and learned doctor to our court./ Where is he?

[d]*Nerissa.* He attendeth here hard by,/ To know your answer, whether you'll admit him.

[e]*Duke.* With all my heart. Some three or four of you/ Go give him courteous conduct to this place./ Meantime the court shall hear Bellario's letter.

[f]*Bellario's Letter.* . . . his own learning, the greatness whereof/ I cannot enough commend, comes with him, at my importunity to/ fill up your Grace's request in my stead.

gracious acceptance, whose trial shall better publish his commendation." [150 *et seq.*]

Enter YOUNG LAWYER.[a]

The Court. "You are welcome: take your place." [170] Are you fully acquainted with the case at bar?[b]

Young Lawyer. I am, your Honor,[c] for Sir Francis Bacon acquainted me "with the cause in controversy[30] between the Jew and Antonio the merchant: we turned o'er many books together . . ."[31] [156] He furnished me with his opinion.[d,32] "Which is the merchant here, and which the Jew?" [174]

The Court. Have the defendant and the plaintiff both rise.[e]

Young Lawyer. "Is your name Shylocke?" [176]

Shylocke. I am the plaintiff. My name is Shylocke.[f]

Young Lawyer. This is a most unusual suit you have brought; yet, by the common law of England, you are within your rights[33] and if you press your suit, you will prevail.[g] And you, my good sir, you are the defendant in this suit, are you not?[h]

Antonio. "Ay, so he says." [181]

Young Lawyer. Do you admit that you executed the bond[34] on which this suit is brought?[i]

Antonio. "I do." [182]

Young Lawyer. Our only hope then, in this court,[35] is that we can induce the plaintiff to be merciful.[j]

Shylocke. "On what compulsion must I? tell me that." [183]

Young Lawyer. "The quality of mercy[36] is not strain'd,
It droppeth as the gentle rain from heaven[37]
Upon the place beneath: it is twice blest;
It blesseth him that gives and him that takes:
'Tis mightiest in the mightiest: it becomes
The throned monarch better than his crown;
His sceptre shows the force of temporal power,
The attribute to awe and majesty,
Wherein doth sit the dread and fear of kings;
But mercy is above this sceptred sway;
It is enthroned in the hearts of kings,
It is an attribute to God himself;

---

[a]*Enter* PORTIA *dressed like a doctor of laws.*

[b]*Duke.* Are you acquainted with the difference/ That holds this present question in the court?

[c]*Portia.* I am informed thoroughly of the cause.

[d]*Bellario's Letter.* . . . he is furnished with my opinion. . . .

[e]*Duke.* Antonio and old Shylocke, both stand forth.

[f]*Shylocke.* Shylocke is my name.

[g]*Portia.* Of a strange nature is the suit you follow;/ Yet in such rule that the Venetian law/ Cannot impugn you as you do proceed.

[h]*Portia.* You stand within his danger, do you not?

[i]*Portia.* Do you confess the bond?

[j]*Portia.* Then must the Jew be merciful.

And earthly power doth then show likest God's
When mercy seasons justice. Therefore, Jew,
Though justice be thy plea, consider this,
That, in the course of justice, none of us
Should see salvation: we do pray for mercy;
And that same prayer doth teach us all to render
The deeds of mercy." [184 *et seq.*]

I have made this equitable plea in the hope that I could prevail upon you to dismiss your suit. If you will not, then, by the common law of England, the court must render judgment in your favor.[a]

Shylocke. I'll not dismiss my suit. I'll take the responsibility for my act. All I want is for the law of England to take its course and give me judgment on my bond.[b]

Young Lawyer. Could he not raise sufficient funds to redeem the bond?[c,38]

Bassanio. Yes, I made a valid "tender"[39] of the sum not an hour before you arrived; in fact, it was six thousand ducats that I tendered him and tender him even now.[d] "And I beseech you," [214] make use of every legal device at your command to force this court of law, in this instance, to do a great right[40] even if, to accomplish it, the court must do a little wrong.[e]

Young Lawyer. There is nothing I can do to alter the judgment[41] (decree) * if it becomes final.[42] If we were to attempt such a thing it would be recorded and used as a precedent,[43] and, by the doctrine of *stare decisis*,[44] such a ruling would become the foundation for innumerable erroneous decisions.[f] ". . . it cannot be," [222] for the common law is inflexible;[45] it has crystallized. He must by law have his judgment.

Shylocke. "A Daniel come to judgement! yea, a Daniel!" [223] "O wise young judge how I do honour thee!" [224]

Young Lawyer. "I pray you, let me look upon the bond."[46] [225]

Shylocke. "Here 'tis, . . . , here it is." [226]

[a]*Portia.* I have spoke thus much/ To mitigate the justice of thy plea;/ Which if thou follow, this strict court of Venice/ Must needs give sentence 'gainst the merchant there.

[b]*Shylocke.* My deeds upon my head! I crave the law,/ The penalty and forfeit of my bond.

[c]*Portia.* Is he not able to discharge the money?

[d]*Bassanio.* Yes, here I tender it for him in the court. . . .

[e]*Bassanio.* Wrest once the law to your authority:/ To do a great right, do a little wrong,/ And curb this cruel devil of his will.

[f]*Portia.* . . . There is no power in Venice/ Can alter a decree established:/ 'Twill be recorded for a precedent,/ And many an error by the same example/ Will rush into the state: it cannot be.

---

* This is the only instance in which Shakespeare used "decree" when judgment is the correct legal term in the Court of King's Bench.

Young Lawyer. "Shylocke, there's thrice thy money offer'd thee." [227]

Shylocke. I've sworn to have the penalty[47] of my bond and would not take all the wealth of London in exchange.[a]

Young Lawyer. "Why, this bond is forfeit." [230] The maturity date is past, and the debt unpaid, so the bond is lawfully enforceable and you can have your pound of flesh, even nearest his heart if you desire to enforce your rights; but why not take three times the money and let me tear[48] this thing to bits[b] and thereby cancel it?

Shylocke. "When it is paid according to the tenour."[49] [235] This appears to be a worthy and a learned court. "You know the law." [237] The plaintiff, therefore, demands "by the law" [238] that the case proceed to judgment. No amount of oratory can alter me. The plaintiff rests and relies on his bond.[c]

Antonio. ". . . , I do beseech the court/ to give the judgement." [243]

Young Lawyer. ". . . : You must prepare your bosom for his knife." [245] Where there is a legal wrong and the damages have been liquidated,[50] the law will enforce the liquidated sum to the last farthing.[d]

Shylocke. " 'Tis very true: O wise and upright judge!" [250]

Young Lawyer. I'm sorry, Antonio, but you must "lay bare your bosom." [252]

Shylocke. "Ay, his breast:
So says the bond: doth it not, noble judge?
'Nearest his heart:' those are the very words." [254]

Young Lawyer. "It is so. Are there balance here to weigh the flesh?" [255]

Shylocke. "I have them ready." [256]

Young Lawyer. Did you think also to engage a surgeon at your expense to see that he does not bleed to death?[e]

Shylocke. "Is it so nominated in the bond?" [259]

Young Lawyer. No, it is not specifically expressed; but it is a condition implied in law, that one be pro-

[a]*Shylocke.* An oath, an oath, I have an oath in heaven:/ Shall I lay perjury upon my soul?

[b]*Portia.* Why, this bond is forfeit;/ And lawfully by this the Jew may claim/ A pound of flesh, to be by him cut off/ Nearest the merchant's heart. Be merciful:/ Take thrice thy money; bid me tear the bond.

[c]*Shylocke.* It doth appear you are a worthy judge;/ You know the law, your exposition/ Hath been most sound: I charge you by the law,/ Whereof you are a well-deserving pillar,/ Proceed to judgement: by my soul I swear/ There is no power in the tongue of man/ To alter me: I stay here on my bond.

[d]*Portia.* For the intent and purpose of the law/ Hath full relation to the penalty,/ Which here appeareth due upon the bond.

[e]*Portia.* Have by some surgeon. Shylocke, on your charge,/ To stop his wounds, lest he do bleed to death.

tected in such contracts, even by the common law.[a] The court has asked me to write the judgment since you, Shylocke, have no counsel; for you understand, do you not, that it is the custom for counsel for the successful litigant to write the judgment which the court is to sign. I will prepare the following judgment:[51]

"A pound of that same merchant's flesh is thine: [299]
The court awards it, and the law doth give it." [300]

"And you must cut this flesh from off his breast: [302]
The law allows it, and the court awards it." [303]

Shylocke. That is satisfactory to me. Your Honor, the plaintiff requests the court to enter the judgment so that it can be enforced[52] immediately.[b]

Young Lawyer. "Tarry a little; there is something else." [305] We intend to avail ourselves of the protection of the Court of Chancery;[53] for Lord Ellesmere has heard the plea.[54] That is where I was before the trial and the reason I was late. Lord Ellesmere has already issued a temporary injunction to become effective when, and if,[55] Lord Chief Justice Coke refuses to hear our writ of error.[56]

The Court. Writ of error refused.

Young Lawyer. Shylocke, we give you formal notice of the temporary injunction[57] that has been issued and notify you of the hearing to show cause thereon in the Court of Chancery.*

Shylocke. What is the world coming to? One court says I can have my pound of flesh and yet I am told by this young lawyer that another court has issued an order of some kind forbidding me to enforce my right.[58]

*   *   *

London. A Court of Chancery.[59] A.D. *1597 of the reign of Elizabeth, the thirty-ninth year.*
LORD ELLESMERE, *Chancellor.*

Young Lawyer. My Lord Chancellor, Justice Coke refused a writ of error in Shylocke vs. Antonio and en-

[a] *Portia.* It is not so express'd: but what of that?

[b] *Shylocke.* A sentence!/ Come, prepare!

---

* The refusal of a writ of error and notice of a temporary injunction were the customary steps used to transfer a case to the Courts of Chancery.

tered a judgment for Shylocke which would do irreparable injury[60] to Antonio. We now ask that your temporary injunction[61] be made permanent.[62]

Lord Chancellor. Are you ready to proceed?

Young Lawyer. The plaintiff and the defendant are here.

Lord Chancellor. You may proceed.

Young Lawyer. Let me review the facts in this case: This bond is a mortgage transaction.[63] Antonio is the mortgagor. Shylocke is the mortgagee. Antonio was unable "to discharge the money" before the mortgage was due. If Shylocke takes his "pound of flesh," pledged in the bond, he will then become a mortgagee in possession. Under the equitable doctrine of waste, he will be accountable to Antonio for the destruction of, or use of, a single part of the estate not expressly covered by the bond.*,[64] Shylocke, "Take thy forfeiture"[65] and have your "pound of flesh"; but, my Lord Chancellor, let me warn him; if he sheds "One drop of Christian blood," "nor cut . . . less nor more/ But just a pound of flesh," by the Statute of Gloucester he must pay three times the excess.[66] Let me further warn you, Shylocke, that there are several informer statutes by which "Thou diest" and "thy lands and goods/ Are . . . confiscate/ Unto the state. . . ."[a]

Lord Chancellor. I am persuaded that the defendant, Shylocke, be permanently enjoined from taking "One drop of . . . blood" [310] or "the twentieth part/ Of one poor scruple," [329] more or less than a pound, of Antonio's flesh. Shylocke, this court acts *in personam*,[67] and you must obey its decree or be in contempt of this court[68] and then you will be severely punished. If you show "humbleness," you shall "see the difference of our spirits." [368]

Shylocke. "Is that the law?" [314]

Young Lawyer. Yes. I can show you the very "act" of Parliament[b] and the decisions on this point. I shall also show you, Shylocke, other law that you have never heard of; for when equity takes jurisdiction over an actual "cause in controversy" it retains jurisdiction for all pur-

[a]*Portia.* This bond doth give thee here no jot of blood;/ The words expressly are 'a pound of flesh:'/ Take then thy bond, take thou thy pound of flesh;/ But, in the cutting it, if thou dost shed/ One drop of Christian blood, thy lands and goods/ Are, by the laws of Venice, confiscate/ Unto the state of Venice.

[b]*Portia.* Thyself shalt see the act. . . .

---

* The writer acknowledges his indebtedness to G. W. Keeton, *Shakespeare and His Legal Problems,* p. 19, for this analogy.

poses, until the ultimate decision of all issues in the case.[a],[69]

Shylocke. I accept the offer of three times my bond, made for my release of Antonio.[b]

Friend of Antonio. "Here is the money." [319]

Young Lawyer. Shylocke shall have everything which "the law allows." Be not too hasty. All that the defendant is entitled to is his pound of flesh. Let him take it, but let him not take one particle more, nor one drop of the plaintiff's blood or he shall be at the mercy of the court for contempt of his decree.[c] "Why doth the Jew pause? take thy forfeiture." [335]

Shylocke. "Give me my principal, and let me go." [366]

Friend of Antonio. "I have it ready for thee; here it is." [337]

Young Lawyer. "He hath refused it in the open court: He shall have merely justice and his bond." [339] We have had in the last twenty-five years a series of cases[70] in which it has been held that, even after the maturity of a bond, the debtor could redeem his property by paying the principal and interest to his creditor, if the debtor could show the Chancellor that he would have paid such sum or sums as are "express'd in the condition," "on such a day, in such a place," * had he not been the victim of some unforeseen circumstance or circumstances over which he had no control, such as, for example, that he was set upon by robbers, that he was delayed by fire or flood, that his ships were lost at sea, or that he had been victimized by his creditors. The same is true of mortgages. This right, or privilege if you will, is called by the most recent authorities the equity of redemption.[71] The plaintiff in this case, soon after the maturity of the bond, made, through his friend Bassanio, a valid tender of three or four times the amount of the bond[d] which was refused by the defendant.[e] He could have accepted this tender and allowed the plaintiff to exercise his equity of redemption; for the defendant, even at common law, could accept what he considered sufficient to satisfy his bond, even though it be less than the face amount or the penalty provided for in

* *The Merchant of Venice,* Act I, Scene iii, 147 *et seq.*

[a]*Portia.* Thyself shalt see the act:/ For, as thou urgest justice, be assur'd/ Thou shalt have justice, more than thou desirest.

[b]*Shylocke.* I take this offer, then; pay the bond thrice/ And let the Christian go.

[c]*Portia.* The Jew shall have all justice; soft! no haste:/ He shall have nothing but the penalty. . . ./ Therefore prepare thee to cut off the flesh./ Shed thou no blood, nor cut thou less nor more/ But just a pound of flesh: if thou cut'st more/ Or less than just a pound, be it but so much/ As makes it light or heavy in the substance,/ Or the division of the twentieth part/ Of one poor scruple, nay, if the scale do turn/ But in the estimation of a hair,/ Thou diest and all thy goods are confiscate.

[d]*Bassanio.* Yea, twice the sum: if that will not suffice,/ I will be bound to pay it ten times o'er,/ On forfeit of my hands, my head, my heart. . . .
[e]*Shylocke.* If every ducat in six thousand ducats/ Were in six parts and every part a ducat,/ I would not draw them; I would have my bond.

case of default. The defendant, as we know, has repeatedly refused to accept anything other than the letter of his bond, and consequently has waived[72] his right to the sum tendered.[a] That waiver is now the basis of an equitable estoppel,[73] or, as we say, he is now estopped from asserting the right which he has waived. Furthermore, he cannot now effectively claim that which he has previously asserted was not his to claim; for, after maturity, by the very terms of the bond he was only entitled to the penalty expressed therein.

Shylocke. "Shall I not have barely my principal?" [342]

Young Lawyer. You shall have nothing but the forfeiture to which you are entitled at common law. This forfeit must be taken at your peril[b,74] for in so doing you may be in contempt of a decree of the Lord Chancellor.

Shylocke. "Why, then the devil give him good of it!" [345]

Young Lawyer. "Tarry, Jew:" [346] My Lord Chancellor, the plaintiff, Antonio, has filed a cross action[75] on behalf of the state[76] under the following statute:[c]

"If it be proved against an alien[77]
That by direct or indirect attempts[78]
He seek the life of any citizen,[79]
The party 'gainst the which he doth contrive
Shall seize one half his goods; the other half
Comes to the privy coffer of the state;
And the offender's life lies in the mercy
Of the Duke only, 'gainst all other voice."

[349 *et seq.*]

The defendant, Shylocke, is not a citizen of the state, for he is a Jew; but Antonio, who is a gentile, was born here and, therefore, possesses the necessary qualification of citizenship. Shylocke has attempted both directly and indirectly to take the life of Antonio. Therefore, it is our contention that this cross action, in which Antonio is plaintiff for himself as informer in the name of the state, comes within the purview of this statute.[d] We pray, therefore, that the Lord Chancellor hear this cross action; for by so doing the court will prevent a multi-

[a]*Portia.* He hath refused it in the open court:/ He shall have merely justice and his bond.

[b]*Portia.* Thou shalt have nothing but the forfeiture,/ To be so taken at thy peril, Jew.

[c]*Portia.* The law hath yet another hold on you./ It is enacted in the laws of Venice,/ If it be proved. . .

[d]*Portia.* In which predicament, I say, thou stand'st;/ For it appears, by manifest proceeding,/ That indirectly and directly too/ Thou hast contrived against the very life/ Of the defendant; and thou hast incurr'd/ The danger formerly by me rehearsed. . . .

plicity of suits.[80] This, as you know, and as you have so often declared from this very bench, is one of the chief concerns of the Court of Chancery.

Lord Chancellor. I will hear the plea and, unless the cross defendant has some unusual defense, will issue a decree in favor of the cross plaintiff; for counsel for Antonio has made a very impressive and forceful argument in his client's cause.

Shylocke. I have nothing to say.

Lord Chancellor. Now, Shylocke, you shall see the great difference between law and equity; for, by the statute that you have heard read in this proceeding, your life and one-half of all of your estate are forfeit to the crown and the other half to Antonio, who brought the action in behalf of the state. But I will spare your life, and, upon further consideration, I may even accept a small fine in lieu of the forfeiture of one-half of your estate.[a]

Young Lawyer. Whatever remission you may grant Shylocke so far as the rights of the state are concerned, I understand that the decree will provide, in any event, that one-half of his goods shall be forfeit to Antonio.[b]

> *Shylocke.* "Nay, take my life and all: pardon not that:
> You take my house when you do take the prop
> That doth sustain my house; you take my life
> When you do take the means whereby I live."
> [374 *et seq.*]

Young Lawyer. Let me consult with Antonio, for he who has sought equity should wish to do equity.[c] If it please the Lord Chancellor, Antonio prefers to return good for evil and act in accordance with the dictates of equity and good conscience in this matter. Therefore, he prays the Chancellor to decree that Shylocke create a *use after a use* with one-half of his estate, to which he, Antonio, is entitled, making the said Antonio the first *cestui que use;* the second *use* to become effective on the death of the said Shylocke and thereby pass the legal and equitable estates to his son-in-law, Lorenzo.[81] Antonio prays the Chancellor to decree further that Shylocke create a trust[82] with the remaining one-half of his estate, naming the Chancellor trustee therein, and

[a]*Duke.* That thou shalt see the difference of our spirits,/ I pardon thee thy life before thou ask it:/ For half thy wealth, it is Antonio's;/ The other half comes to the general state,/ Which humbleness may drive unto a fine.

[b]*Portia.* Ay, for the state, not for Antonio.

[c]*Portia.* What mercy can you render him, Antonio?

by the terms of said trust make himself the *cestui que trust*[83] thereof for life.[a]

> *Lord Chancellor.* "He shall do this, or else I do recant The pardon that I late pronounced here."[84] [391]

Young Lawyer. "Art thou contented, Jew? what dost thou say?" [393]

Shylocke. "I am content." [394]

Young Lawyer. "Clerk, draw a deed of gift." [394]

Shylocke. With the Lord Chancellor's permission I shall leave the court now for I am ill. Send the instruments to me that need my signature and I shall sign them.[b]

Lord Chancellor. "Get thee gone, but do it."[85] [397]

[a] *Antonio.* So please my lord the Duke and all the court/ To quit the fine for one half of his goods,/ I am content; so he will let me have/ The other half *in use* (in trust), to render it,/ Upon his death, unto the gentleman/ That lately stole his daughter:/ Two things provided more, that, for this favour,/ He presently become a Christian;/ The other, that he do record a gift,/ Here in the court, of all he dies possess'd,/ Unto his son Lorenzo and his daughter.

[b] *Shylocke.* I pray you, give me leave to go from hence;/ I am not well: send the deed after me,/ And I will sign it.

DECREE[86]

I.

It is ordered, the injunction formerly granted against the defendant for stay of his judgment in the case of Shylocke vs. Antonio in the King's Bench be made permanent; and the defendant be perpetually restrained thereby from enforcing his judgment at law.*

II.

It is decreed, the defendant shall not collect from the plaintiff, or from any one in his behalf, any sum of money or other property in satisfaction of the debt contracted by the plaintiff in the bond, which was the basis of the defendant's cause of action in the King's Bench.

* See note 58, case 3.

III.

It is decreed, the defendant shall, with one-half of his estate, immediately create a *use after a use* in which the plaintiff, Antonio, shall have both the legal and equitable title for the life of Shylocke, and upon the decease of the said Shylocke the legal and equitable title to the property shall pass to the use of Lorenzo, his son-in-law.[87]

IV.

It is decreed, the defendant shall, with the remaining one-half of his estate, create at once a trust, naming the Chancellor as trustee, in which he himself shall be the beneficiary[88] for life. Upon his death the trustee shall convey[89] the corpus of the trust in fee to Jessica, the daughter of the creator of the trust, and her husband, Lorenzo, and their heirs.[90]

v.

In issuing this decree the Chancellor has been influenced solely by the pleadings and evidence submitted on this hearing and, therefore, only the issues so raised are determined by this decree. It shall remain for a later cause to determine the significance of such issues as fraud and misrepresentation at the execution of a contract or bond; and the much greater issue of the relation of such heinous contracts to the public policy of the state.

Part II

The authorities are covered with dust of three centuries and two score years; but we shall attempt to glean, from the law French* of pages yellowed with age, the story of the living law without distorting the comedies and tragedies written there, of those who little realized that their current problems were to mold the lives and destinies of future generations who were to live in centuries yet unborn, from ages not yet conceived.

---

* Law French is partly the Latin of Julius Caesar, partly the French of William the Conqueror, and partly the English of Geoffrey Chaucer. In its many variations, it is the language of English jurisprudence until the fifteenth century.

Queen Elizabeth

1. Shakespeare, in *The Merchant of Venice,* is expounding English jurisprudence, not Roman civil law.

I do not hesitate to change the venue[A] of this trial from Venice to London, for I hope to convince the reader, as this work progresses, that the procedure of the trial and the substantive law expressed therein are so definitely a part of English jurisprudence that the case of Shylocke vs. Antonio could not have been tried before any forum other than the Court of King's Bench[B] and the Court of Chancery[C] sitting at Westminster, a city on the Thames near London.

The customary practice has been to retain the scene of the trial in Venice and then prove or disprove the authenticity of the law therein depicted by English authorities. The inconsistency of this method of procedure should appear at once for, if the trial is in Venice and the bond written there, the law applicable to the case is the civil law of Rome, and the authorities should be taken from that great system of law and should conform to the Code Justinian.

E. J. White, in his *Commentaries on the Law in Shakespeare,* takes issue with Lord Campbell's statement: "To Shakespeare's law, lavishly as he propounds it, there can neither be demurrer, nor bill of exception, nor writ of error" and says:

But of this, at all times, it may be doubted if the statement is not too general, for sometimes, for dramatic effect, or under the license of poetry, the law is not correctly presented, as in the trial scene of the "Merchant of Venice," where illegal reasons are assigned for giving judgment against Shylock. No scientific lawyer could have written this play and delivered the judgment that Portia is made to deliver, in denying Shylock his pound of flesh.

However, in the main, the law presented in the plays is accurately written and correctly used.

It is my contention that the reasons "assigned for giving judgment against Shylock" are not "illegal" but are equitable.

I do not understand why Mr. White failed to see this point from the following argument, cited by him with approval in *his own* book:

Mr. Davis, in his commentaries on the "Law in Shakespeare" observes that *the Poet might very properly have invoked the chancery process of injunction to relieve against the enforcement of this penalty of the bond,* as this procedure was then recognized by the English Court of Chancery, but of course if this were true—which the history of the Chancery Court establishes—an English Court would have had no jurisdiction of an action in a Venetian State, so this observation would not have furnished the Poet with a much better remedy than the subterfuge he adopted to let Antonio escape from the obligation of his bond.[D]

The author *then proceeds* to prove the points of law, as they arise in the play, by *English common law* (not by Venetian law) as shown by these passages appearing on the next and following pages of his book.

Sec. 88. Seal.—

"*Shy.* Till thou can'st rail the seal from off my bond, Thou but offend'st thy lungs to speak so loud."

[A] Sir Edward Coke, *Institutes of the Laws of England; or, a Commentary upon Littleton: Not the Name of the Author only, but of the Law Itself,* Vol. I, Sect. 193. Lat. *visentum,* neighborhood. The word was formerly spelled *visne.*

[B] See note 2.

[C] See note 13.

[D] E. J. White, *Commentaries on the Law in Shakespeare,* pp. 123–124.

In these lines Shylock expressed the preference that his debt held, under the English law, because of the seal attached, over debts not so evidenced. A bond or other writing, under seal, was called a specialty contract, to distinguish it from other writings or contracts, not bearing a seal. A specialty debt, such as a bond under seal, in the event of the debtor's death, prior to 1870, when such preference was abolished, had the right of prior payment over simple contract debts.[A]

Sec. 99. Effect of legal precedent—

"*Por.* It must not be; there is no power in Venice
Can alter a decree established:
'Twill be recorded for a precedent;
And many an error by the same example,
Will rush into the state: it cannot be."

The Poet here refers to the doctrine of *stare decisis,* and the sacredness of established precedents in the law, which have been truly said to be the real "bulwarks" of the law. From the time of Edward III to that of Elizabeth, the inviolability of established precedents was inculcated by the courts and lawyers with more zeal, perhaps, than at any other period in English history.[B]

It is not the intent of the writer to single out Mr. White from those who have written upon this subject but to treat his work as typical of an earlier form of Shakespearean criticism.

For a scholarly and illuminating discussion of some of the legal and equitable principles involved in this shift of scene, see Hazeltine's introduction to Turner's *The Equity of Redemption,* entitled "The Roman *Fiducia cum Creditore* and the English Mortgage, A Comparison With Special Reference to the Right of Redemption."

2. *A court of justice.*

The following is the briefest possible description of the rock whence Shakespeare's "court of justice" was hewn and the hole of the pit whence it was digged.

Before the advent of William the Conqueror, the affairs of the ordinary inhabitant of England were administered by local assemblies scattered throughout the island, while the disputes of the privileged few were settled by the King and his witan. From this witan, William I developed the Magnum Concilium which was composed of the King's tenants in chief, his important officials, and others whose personal service and assistance he desired. This, therefore, was a very large and unwieldy body which of necessity had to be divided, and the powers of which had to be delegated. In this process the King rather strengthened than lessened his power, for he was thrown into bolder relief as the titular head of a continuously centralizing state. In addition to the Magnum Concilium, and somewhat a part of it, was the Curia Regis which was, in effect, a quasi standing committee. Two of the first significant offshoots from this main trunk of jurisprudence were the justices in Eyre and the itinerant justices. The former attended to judicial matters that were more pertinent to the welfare of the state, such as the examination of the tax rolls and collection of information for the *Domesday Book;* and the latter, or itinerant justices, assumed the duties of judicial decision and soon developed regular itineraries which became known to prospective litigants. The esteem for these itinerant justices, on the part of the ordinary citizen, was far different from the hatred they bore the justices in Eyre who saw to it that the last penny in taxes was wrung from them. In 1178, as a result of popular demand and necessity, one place in the realm was se-

---

[A] *Ibid.,* pp. 125–126.
[B] *Ibid.,* pp. 137–138.

lected where one of these itinerant justices should always be holding court. The place selected was Westminster, a small city on the Thames. This permanent court was given the unassuming title of Court of Common Pleas. It decided cases between citizens, as distinguished from Pleas of the Crown; that is, cases in which the King was involved. Questions of great weight and difficulty were referred to the King for decision by him and by those who were retained in the Curia Regis. This Court of Common Pleas had exclusive jurisdiction of those disputes arising from the ownership and conveyance of land, and a theoretical monopoly of the personal actions of debt, detinue, covenant, account, and trespass. The men selected to hear cases of unusual difficulty and great importance gained for themselves the title of Court of King's Bench.

When Shakespeare wrote *The Merchant of Venice* there were the following judicial forums, of various origin, in England in which his contemporaries might or might not be able to sue or be sued: Quarter Sessions, Justice of the Peace Courts, Itinerant Justices or Assize Courts, Court of Common Pleas, Court of King's Bench (then the Court of Queen's Bench), Court of Exchequer Chamber, Court of Admiralty, Court of Chancery, and even the House of Lords.[A]

3. A.D. 1597.

The Merchant of Venice was written before 1598, for it is one of the six comedies specifically mentioned by Meres in his *Palladis Tamia* in 1598. It was very probably written after 1596 for in that year Sylvain's *Orator*, a book which contained part of the argument of the bond plot, was published in English translation; thus, the conclusion that the play was presented for the first time late in the year 1596 or in 1597.

4. Sir Edward Coke, Lord Chief Justice of the King's Bench.

If I were asked to name the three men in all England who were most profoundly affected by Shakespeare's *The Merchant of Venice,* I should unhesitatingly name the following: Sir Edward Coke, Sir Thomas Egerton, later to become Lord Ellesmere, and Sir Francis Bacon. This statement is made after due consideration, for these three men were to English jurisprudence of the late sixteenth and early seventeenth centuries what Shakespeare, Marlowe, and Johnson were to Elizabethan drama; and *The Merchant of Venice* was the one instance in which jurisprudence and drama came together *vis-a-vis*.

Two of the three men whom I have named were approximately the age of Shakespeare, and Lord Ellesmere was his senior by twenty-three years. They were outstanding figures at the end of the sixteenth century, and it was they who enacted the legal drama which corrected what Blackstone chose to call a "solecism." Each probably saw this play, and two of them in the most outstanding moments of their careers used language that is a clear echo of Shakespeare's immortal lines in *The Merchant of Venice*.[B]

[A] The writer is indebted to E. M. Morgan, *Introduction to the Study of Law*, pp. 1–26, for the essence of this note.

[B] See note 16.

Anno 1629.

PATIENS · PRVDENS · QVI

JPayne fecit

Sir Edward Coke

I say they were most profoundly affected by the play, for each must have realized that he was seeing depicted before his very eyes the folly of the situation in which the courts had become involved and at least one plausible indication of a solution thereto. They may also have realized that they, because of their professional prominence and the official positions which they occupied, were destined to play the leading roles in the legal counterpart of the dramatic case of Shylocke vs. Antonio.

Act IV, Scene i, of the play does not depict a legal quibble, as is often said, but is a profound study of the greatest judicial problem of English jurisprudence which was at its controversial height when *The Merchant of Venice* was written. Much later, Blackstone writing of this problem in his commentary describes it as follows:

> . . . and sure there cannot be a greater solecism, than that in two sovereign independent courts established in the same country, exercising concurrent jurisdiction, and over the same subject matter, there should exist in a single instance two different rules of property, clashing with or contradicting each other.[A]

This problem was whether an injunction of the Court of Chancery could issue and be effective against the enforcement of a judgment of the common law courts: whether law or equity should be supreme.

Let us now determine the position of Coke, Ellesmere, and Bacon in 1597. Each of them was living in London and was a member of the Inns of Court. Sir Francis Bacon was one of the most active and outstanding members of Gray's Inn when Shakespeare's *The Comedy of Errors* was presented there.

Lord Ellesmere, in 1596, was appointed Lord Keeper of the Great Seal, a title bestowed by the Queen on the Lord Chancellor of the Court of Chancery. He would therefore have been one of the jurists before whom Antonio's case would have been tried had it been an actual "cause in controversy." (156) [B]

Sir Francis Bacon was fast gaining recognition as a great lawyer and in 1594 was engaged in a most important case involving the judicial interpretation of the Statute of Uses,[C] known as Chudleigh's Case.[D] In January, 1597, he published his *Essays* which assured his lasting fame. He was a follower of the Earl of Essex and was keenly interested in the social and economic life of Elizabethan London. Sir Francis Bacon, no doubt, would have been the barrister whose services Antonio would have engaged and to whom, before the year 1598, the Lord Chief Justice might have turned as *Amicus Curiae*. It is not strange, therefore, that it was he on whom James I relied to solve the seeming impasse into which, in 1616, Lord Ellesmere and Sir Edward Coke found themselves—in a case involving the same legal and equitable principles as those contained in and illustrated by Antonio's case.

One of the members of this legal triumvirate, Sir Edward Coke, was born in Milihom in Norfolk on the first day of February, 1552, and was therefore Shakespeare's senior by twelve years. He was the son of a prosperous barrister and never knew the want of money as did his rival,

---

[A] Sir William Blackstone, *Commentaries on the Laws of England,* Book III, p. 1395.

[B] William Shakespeare, *The Merchant of Venice.* All line numbers refer to the Globe text.

[C] *Year Books,* 27 Henry VIII, c. 10, Chudleigh's Case (1535–1536).

[D] Sir Edward Coke, *The Reports of Sir Edward Coke,* Part I, pp. 113–141.

Sir Francis Bacon. He too was a graduate of Trinity College, Cambridge, and then, *mirabile dictu,* this greatest of all common law judges attended not one of the Inns of Law but Clifford's Inn—one of the Inns of Chancery. Coke remained there only one year, however, and the following year—1579—transferred his activities to the Inner Temple where he soon showed his great genius for the law and its subtle arguments.

In 1581, this young barrister, not yet thirty, took an active part as counsel for the successful litigant in Shelley's case,[A] one of the foundation stones of the English and American law of real property.

By 1592, Coke had reached the zenith of his profession and, in search of new outlets for his tremendous intellect, turned to the field of political jurisprudence. His efforts were rewarded, for in 1594 he was appointed to the office of Attorney General, and thus began a rivalry with a younger aspirant for that office—Sir Francis Bacon —that was destined to continue throughout their lives.

Promotion followed promotion, from that of Judge of the Court of Common Pleas in 1606 to the most exalted position offered by the common law, Lord Chief Justice, a title used in addressing Coke when he presided over the Court of King's Bench in 1613.

Thus, at the time Shakespeare was penning the lines of the dramatic trial scene of *The Merchant of Venice* or soon thereafter, we find Sir Edward Coke assuming the role of champion of the cause of the common law in its struggle for judicial

supremacy with equity, sponsored by Sir Thomas Egerton (later to become Lord Ellesmere) and Sir Francis Bacon, the lawyer and philosopher, in a case destined to produce a synthesis and thereby bring order out of chaos and for all time to eliminate the possibility of the situation in which Shylocke found himself.

If we turn for a moment to a more personal and lighter vein in the lives of Coke and Bacon, and consequently ignore position and title, we find that Lord Ellesmere and his Court of Chancery were the predestined victors over Lord Chief Justice Coke and the common law, as shown by the following quotation:

> On 27th June, 1598, his [Coke's] first wife died, but he was soon consoled. He, with Bacon and others, sought the hand of Lady Hatton, a young widow of twenty, and grand-daughter of Burleigh, who had a very large fortune. In spite of Coke's age and unattractive personal appearance, he was the succesful suitor. . . . The marriage was not a success, and Bacon was consoled by opportunities he had of assisting Lady Coke in her incessant disputes with her husband, which became a matter of public notoriety.[B]

Could personal rivalry and animosity have been contributing causes in Bacon's decision in favor of Lord Ellesmere?[C]

5. ". . . is Antonio here?"

From the case of William Gardner vs. Edward Walshe, citizen and leatherseller of London, which was tried in 1586 in the Michaelmas Term of Queen's Bench and

---

[A] *Ibid.,* pp. 88–106.

[B] The Earl of Birkenhead, *Fourteen English Judges,* p. 29.

[C] *Ibid.* The writer hereby acknowledges his indebtedness for the essence of this note.

reported in *King's Bench Reports*, 27, 1299, p. 147, I quote only the following passages which show the necessity of the appearance of the defendant in person, or by counsel, before it is possible to begin a suit at common law:

> . . . the sheriffs are to produce the said Edward in the said Chancery on the Quindene of St. Michael next, to say why the money had not be [been] raised on his lands and goods according to the form and effect of the recognizance.
>
> On which Quindene of St. Michael the sheriffs of Middlesex returned the writ saying that the aforesaid Edward was dead. Whereupon another writ was directed to the sheriff of Surrey to bring the heirs and tenants of the said Edward into Chancery on the Octave of St. Martin next.
>
> The sheriff of Surrey returned that by virtue of the said writ, on 26 November 27 Eliz. (1585) he had made known to Richard Ryther, James Chiwall and Lawrence Browne, the tenants of the said Edward, that they should be at Westminster on the day, etc. . . .
>
> On the Octave of St. Hilary 28 Eliz. (1585/6) the said William, Richard, James and Lawrence came by their attorneys, etc.[A]

Thus, the judge by his first words, "What, is Antonio here?" [1], was contemplating the fulfillment of a condition precedent to the trial of a suit at common law, namely, the presence of the defendant and Antonio's announcement, "Ready, so please your grace."

6. ". . . no lawful means can carry me/Out of his envy's reach. . . ."

Thus, at the outset, Shakespeare reassures his audience that there was no defense at common law to Shylocke's bond under seal.

[A] Leslie Hotson, *Shakespeare versus Shallow*, pp. 219–220.

7. "I have not a half-penny to spend on a pleader. . . ."

It has been the custom of the common law from its very inception to permit one to act as his own counsel, whether he be plaintiff or defendant; and I need not point out the fact that Shylocke had no counsel. For centuries, only those having special training and possessing certain qualifications have been allowed to represent others. Thus, we have Antonio represented by the learned young protege of Bellario for the major part of the trial, while Shylocke pleads his own cause. The earliest records indicate that it has been the court's duty to appoint counsel for an impecunious defendant and to be more lenient in its enforcement of the strict rules of procedure when a litigant, by choice or necessity, acts as his own counsel. During the reign of Elizabeth, and especially prior thereto, litigants often pleaded their own causes, and the court quite frequently, and in a most informal manner, advised them, as shown by the following cases:

The plaintiff, Alice, first tells in her own way how she has been seduced by the defendant, Thomas, and then asks for a remedy at law as follows:

> Alice can get no justice at all, seeing that she is poor and this Thomas is rich. Think of me, sir, for God's sake and for the Queen's soul's sake. [Book 2, Select Bills in Eyre (Shropshire Eyre, A.D. 1292), 2.][B]

John Feyrewyn pleaded his case thus:

> Dear sir, I cry mercy of you who are put in the place of our lord the King to do right to the poor and the rich. As soon, my lord, as I get my money, I will go to the Holy Land, and there I will pray

---

[B] Morgan, *op. cit.*, p. 10.

for the King of England and for you especially, Sir John of Berewick, for I tell you I have not a halfpenny to spend on a pleader; and so for this, dear sir, be gracious unto me that I may get my money back. [Book 2, Select Bills in Eyre (Shropshire Eyre, A.D. 1292), 6.][A]

8. Withdrawal of suit by *Nolle Prosequi*.

In the case of W.G. vs. T.N. and J.T., citizens and scriveners of London, which is reported in *King's Bench Reports*, 27, 1366, p. 225 and was tried in 1596 at the Hilary Term of the Queen's Bench, the plaintiff alleged that he had bought for £420 the following jewels:

. . . one "honye combe of golde", "one booke and one coller of golde", the coller containing 20 "buttons" of which six are set with "a Dyamonde a peece", nine with two "pearles a peece", four with "one rubye a peece", "the other lacking hys stone", and the book set with 14 "Rubyes", 14 "Turkeys", and 2 "Saphers," weighing together 14 ounce. . . . "one rynge sett wth fower diamondes;" . . . provided that if on or before 21 January next after the date of the writing they paid Gardiner £420 at the shop of the said John Thompson in Cornhill, that then the sale should be void.[B]

The plaintant, G., then claimed that he had not received the £420 on the designated day and, therefore, was entitled to all of the jewels and the £600 penalty in the bond. N. and T. replied that the sum was paid at the appointed time and place. The case was set for trial on February 11, 1596, but G. did not appear and thus, in effect, withdrew his suit by failure to prosecute it to judgment. If G. could have produced the bond he could have kept the

jewels and had judgment for the penalty, regardless of the evidence of payment produced by N. and T. even though the court was certain of the injustice of the judgment; thus was the severity of the law in Shakespeare's day.[C]

9. "I have possess'd your grace of what I purpose; . . . ."

The following petition, which was filed in the Michaelmas Term, 38 Elizabeth, is quite brief but most apropos:

Anglia ss Willelmus Wayte petit securitates pacis versus Willelmum Shakspere, Franciscum Langley, Dorotheam Soer uxorem Johannis Soer, & Annam Lee, ob metum mortis &c.

Attachiamentum vicecomiti Surreie retornabile xviii Martini.[D]

An idiomatic translation of this legal Latin is as follows: England. Be it known that the plaintiff in this cause, the said William Wayte, petitions this court to have sureties of the peace appointed for William Shakespeare, the defendant in the above entitled and numbered cause, and also for Francis Langley, Dorothy Soer, wife of one John Soer, and Anne Lee; for the said defendants have threatened, and continue to threaten, the life of the said plaintiff, who, thereby, is in fear of death or grave bodily harm.

Wherefore the plaintiff prays that a writ of attachment issue to the sheriff of Surrey, returnable on the eighteenth of St. Martin, that being the last day of this term, and that the said plaintiff William Wayte re-

---

[A] *Ibid.*
[B] Hotson, *op. cit.*, pp. 302–303.

[C] See also note 45.
[D] Hotson, *op. cit.*, p. 9.

ceive judgment against William Shakespeare *et al.* in the said cause.[A]

This bit of concrete evidence shows, beyond a doubt, that Shakespeare had heard one other than Shylocke "possess" the court of what he "purposed" and, therefore, knew whereof he spoke.

10. ". . . let the danger light Upon your charter. . . ."

The rivalry between the common law courts and the chancery courts, while the keenest, was not the only judicial rivalry in 1597, for the Courts of Admiralty were also very popular, and, contrary to the wishes of the common law judges who were anxious to have admiralty jurisdiction limited to contracts made *super altum mare*, these courts continued to hear cases arising not only out of disputes on the high seas but also those between merchants. In order not to lose this litigation to the Court of Admiralty, the common law judges prevailed upon the crown to enlarge their jurisdiction by special charter. Thus, they obtained jurisdiction of the commercial relations of merchants. This "law merchant" was a new field for the common lawyers who soon realized that their rules were too inflexible to meet the manifold situations confronting them. Therefore, they urged upon the court the policy of giving judicial recognition to the well-established customs of merchants. This practice became so extensive that one William West published a collection of such precedents in 1615, which was "Newly augmented with divers Presidents touching

Merchant's affairs." These "Presidents" include those relating to charter parties,[B] bills of lading,[C] bills of exchange,[D] bonds, negotiable instruments, and merchant's marks (trademarks).[E]

The following dialogue indicates that the struggle between the "law merchant" and the common law was of an early origin, as was that between law and equity:

> Mettingham, C. J. He who demands this debt is a merchant; and therefore if he can give slight proof to support his tally we will incline to that side.— Goesfield, Alas! Sir we are at common law; wherefore we are advised that he shall not be received in court, in as much as he can have his recovery elsewhere by Law Merchant.[F]

The common law courts finally absorbed so many of these precedents of the businessmen of England that Coke said the law merchant was a part of the common law.[G] The common law judges were anxious to keep this law merchant a part of the law of the realm, and it was this, and not municipal charters, that Shylocke had in mind when he threatened the judge with these words,

[I have sworn to] have the due and forfeit of my bond:
If you deny it, let the danger light
Upon your charter and your city's freedom.[H]
[36 *et seq.*]

[A] *Ibid.* The writer acknowledges his indebtedness for the essence of this translation.

[B] Coke, *Reports* . . . , Vol. VI, p. 48A.

[C] 1 Browne & G. 22.

[D] *The English Reports*, Vol. 79 (King's Bench Division, Book VIII), p. 262.

[E] *Ibid.*, p. 402, per Doderedge J.

[F] *Year Books*, 21–22 Edward I, plea 13.

[G] Coke, . . . *a Commentary upon Littleton* . . . , p. 182A: ". . . and this is *per legem mercatoriam*, which (as hath been said) is part of the lawes of this realm."

[H] For an interesting early discussion of this subject, see Wyndham Beawes, *Lex Mercatoria Rediviva: or, a complete Code of Commercial Law, being a General Guide to all Men in Business.*

11. ". . . the trade and profit of the city consisteth of all nations."

One of the earliest rules of the common law was that no man could convey better title to goods than that which he himself possessed. Consequently, one who bought goods always faced the danger that they were stolen and, therefore, must be surrendered to the true owner who claimed them.

For centuries, London had been one of the chartered cities where free trade was allowed. These centers of trade and commerce were called free cities or Markets-Overt, i.e., this strict rule of the common law was not applied to transactions occurring in the markets of London.[A] By the decisions of the common law courts, the precedent was established that the purchaser of goods in a Market-Overt acquired a valid and marketable title to them, regardless of the validity of the title of the vendor. Similar precedents had developed as to bonds and negotiable contracts, and thus had evolved a custom that was of great value to merchants who, in the hurry and bustle of Elizabethan trade, could not take time to investigate the validity of the title to all the goods they purchased. This matter of the Market-Overt—the freedom of trade in London—was of the utmost importance and was one of the topics most discussed, for there was not complete unanimity of opinion on this subject since these "open" markets were a great inducement to thievery. This current controversy, like many others, was finally settled by a lawsuit, which Coke must have thought of great importance, for in his reports he gave

---

[A] *Ibid.*

it the title "Case of Market-Overt," rather than designating it by the names of the litigants. This case is reported in Coke, *Reports,* Part V, p. 83, and was tried at "Hillary term in the reign of Elizabeth the 38 year (1596) ."

This famous case, establishing the "city's freedom," was decided a few months before the play was written. Is it not reasonable to assume that the reference in the play is to it and that the members of the audience were aware of the reference?

Is it not significant that we find Shakespeare's Shylocke threatening this court by saying that to give him any less than the full penalty of his bond would be a step in retreat from this recent victory of the businessman and once more shake their faith in the validity of bonds and title to goods acquired in the free markets of London? Antonio's words are an appropriate answer to the question:

The duke cannot deny the course of law:
for the commodity that strangers have
With us in Venice, if it be denied,
Will much impeach the justice of his state;
Since that the trade and profit of the city
Consisteth of all nations. . . .

[Act III, scene iii, 26 et seq.]

The following is Coke's report of the case:

At the Sessions of Newgate now last past, it was resolv'd by *Popham* Chief Justice of *England,* *Anderson* Ch. Justice of the Common Pleas, Sir Thomas Egerton [Lord Ellesmere] Master of the Rolls, the Attorney General, and the Court, That if Plate be stolen and sold openly in a Scrivener's Shop on the Market-Day, (as every Day is a (*a*) Market-Day in *London* except (*b*) Sunday) that this Sale should not change the Property, but the Party should have Restitution; for a (*c*) Scrivener's Shop is not a Market-overt for Plate; for none would search there for such a Thing; *etc. sic de similibus,* etc. But if the Sale had been openly in a

(d) Goldsmith's Shop in *London,* so that any one that stood or passed by the Shop might see it, there it would change the Property.[A]

12. ". . . I'll not answer that. . . ."

James Bradley Thayer calls attention to Shakespeare's strict adherence to the law of evidence, as it was in the reign of Richard II (1377–99), in the following terms:

So it was with "trial by battle" in our old law; the issue of right, in a writ of right, including all elements of law and fact, was "tried" by this physical struggle, and the judges of the Common Pleas sat, like the referee at a prize-fight, simply to administer the procedure, the rules of the game. So of the King's Bench in criminal appeals; and so sat Richard II at the trial of the appeal of treason between Bolingbroke and Norfolk, as Shakespeare represents it in the play.[B]

This allusion to Shakespeare is given a very significant stamp of approval by the fact that it is quoted *in toto* by Wigmore, the greatest modern authority on the law of evidence.[C]

The development of the law of evidence from Richard II to Elizabeth was quite rapid, and when Shakespeare put the words quoted above into the mouth of Shylocke he was exemplifying the law of the admissibility of relevant evidence in 1597. I have selected the following quotation to illustrate the great strides that this branch of the law had made during the intervening two hundred years:

If a man be robbed or wounded and he writes down a *perfect* description of the men whereby they are known and so dies, this will be good evidence to convict them.[D]

This is most significant of the changes that the common law was undergoing in order to compete with the Court of Chancery.

13. The Court of Chancery.

The same jealousy and shortsightedness of the common law courts that caused the creation of the Court of Chancery continued to feed the fires of the struggle between the opposing forces of law and equity for approximately three and one-half centuries.

The common law courts, as I have shown, sprang from the Curia Regis; but the Court of Chancery had an entirely different origin. It evolved from the council and the King, who was considered the fountainhead of all law.

The early Chancellors, under Henry III, performed the service of issuing writs to litigants. This was the only method of entertaining a lawsuit, and the Chancellor did not hesitate to issue these writs in slightly varying forms so that gradually new forms of action began to develop. These novel suits increased the duties of the already overburdened law judges who complained to the King. As a result of these complaints, the Chancellor was forbidden to issue any writ that did not conform exactly to the five or six common law forms of action which were known and recognized as such. Thus, until some new method could be devised, access to the courts was restricted to certain very specific types of injury.

[A] Coke, *Reports* . . . , Part V, p. 83.

[B] James Bradley Thayer, "Presumptions and the Law of Evidence," "Law and Fact in Jury Trials," *Harvard Law Review,* III, 143, 4 id. 156.

[C] J. H. Wigmore, *Evidence in Trials at Common Law,* Vol. I, Ch. II, Sect. 9.

[D] Coke, *Reports* . . . , p. 318.

The social and economic necessity for litigation increased to such an extent, due to this damming of the judicial stream, that a few of the more daring citizens sought relief from the King, whom many had always looked upon as the true source of all "justice" and "mercy." To use the words of E. M. Morgan, "He petitioned the King or the King in Council, or the King in Parliament, because his case was unusual, or his opponent was too powerful, *or the offense too heinous,* or the subject matter too difficult, *or the usual remedies inadequate.*"[A]

Once more the King turned to the Chancellor, who knew most about the issuance of these special writs, and again the common law judges protested and often, on motion of the defendant, quashed such writs as unwarranted and invalid at common law. Edward III appreciated the heretofore untapped source of revenue in these special writs and, therefore, authorized his Chancellor to issue them to all whom he deemed worthy, without the King's special approbation. Thus, we find the Chancellor invested with unlimited power to issue writs in any form that he desired to any applicant, and the common law judges were invested with a like power to nullify the effect of such writs by quashing them. The Chancellor decided, about 1350, to overcome this impasse by hearing the cases on these special writs himself. This was the first distinct separation of law from equity. From that year until the matter was settled in 1616, there was an ever-increasing battle for supremacy. Once more the combatant possessing agile, swift-moving, self-adapting faculties was destined to be victorious over a powerful,

stately but ponderous adversary, just as the English yeomanry defeated the flower of chivalry at Agincourt, and the light and easily handled craft of the Elizabethans defeated the great unmanageable men of war that comprised the Spanish Armada. As I have said, equity was the predestined victor, but let us watch the struggle and see if we can determine what effect it had upon the trial scene of *The Merchant of Venice* and, what is just as fascinating and interesting, the effect that the dramatic trial had upon the actual shaping of events.

The Chancellor, now that there was a tribunal where cases on special writs could be heard, became very popular; and his office, in many respects, was second to no other. Since the cases before him were all very unusual and involved difficult and distressing problems, and since he was not burdened with a jury, the procedure in chancery differed greatly from the procedure in the law courts; and, what is most important of all, the Chancellor was unfettered and was, therefore, guided and moved by the facts of the particular case before him.

He did not hesitate to depart from long-established legal principles, and "To do a great right, do a little wrong." (216) He often balanced the equities, which is the prosaic counterpart of the line just quoted. The Chancellor was always guided by the doctrines of Christianity and administered "rules of equity and good conscience" which seemed so elastic and indefinite to the common law judges that Selden called chancery "a rougish thing" because it had no measure more constant than the Chancellor's foot.[B]

[A] Morgan, *op. cit.,* p. 11. The italics are the writer's.

[B] The writer is indebted to Morgan, *op. cit.,* pp. 1–26, for the essence of this note.

The Chancellors very wisely decided to preserve written reports of their decisions, so that there would be some general idea of the size of the preceding Chancellor's feet or at least records to show that he had his judicial feet on the ground; and when Shylocke sued Antonio in 1597, and Antonio appealed ultimately to the Chancellor because of the "peculiar and heinous nature of his case," the Chancellor could refer to the precedent of reported cases for a century. And, to use Selden's disdainful allusion once more, he was not bound by the exact size of the shoe of any of his predecessors and, therefore, in selecting a shoe to fit the case of Shylocke vs. Antonio, had many different sizes to select from so that he could find a shoe to fit both the left and right foot of each party to the hearing and was not restricted, as the common law judge, to one size shoe for all litigants.

14. The Judicature Act.

In 1873, Parliament passed the Supreme Court of Judicature or Judicature Act, which consolidated the great English courts situated at Westminster into one Supreme Court of Judicature and established a uniform law of procedure therefor.[A] By this act, so far as procedure is concerned, the courts of common law and equity were merged; but the spirit of the two, differences of viewpoint, and method of solution of judicial problems remain. And today, as in the time of Shakespeare, equity is the refuge from those who seek their "pound of flesh."

[A] *The Law Reports,* Vol. VIII, Ch. 66, p. 306.

15. Lord Chancellor Ellesmere.

There is more than the usual amount of legend and tradition surrounding the early life of Sir Thomas Egerton, Lord Ellesmere. These are the facts we know: The natural son of Sir Richard Egerton and a Miss Sparks, he was born in the parish of Doddleston in the year 1540 and was acknowledged by his father to whom he was indebted for his education at Brasenose College, Oxford. He was a most diligent and worthy student who showed, at an early age, his unusual aptitude for the law. According to the following tradition, he was, while still in college, a believer in those equitable principles which he championed all of his life and which he beheld triumphant just before his death, for it was he who marshalled the forces of equity in the last campaign against the common law courts under Judge Coke, which, I am convinced, was one of the inspirations for the particular form of the trial scene, as we have it, in *The Merchant of Venice:*

It is related that he [Lord Ellesmere] first gave earnest of his future eminence by interposing as *Amicus Curiae,* while yet a student, when a verdict was about to be pronounced which would have ruined a worthy old lady who kept a house of public entertainment in Smithfield. Three graziers had deposited a sum of money with her, to be returned to them on their joint application. One of them, fraudulently pretending that he had authority to receive it, induced her to give him the whole of the money and absconded with it. The other two brought their action against her; and (as the story goes) were about to recover, when young Egerton begged permission to befriend the Court by pointing out a fatal objection which had escaped her Counsel as well as my Lord Judge. Said he: "This money, by the contract, was to be returned to *three* but *two* only sue;—where is the *third?* let him appear with the others; till then the money can not be demanded from her." This turned the for-

HONORATISS . D^{no} . THOMAS EGERTONUS BARO DE ELLESMER ANGLIÆ CANCELLA^{ri9}

Virtutis quicunque oculo vis cernere formam:
Ecce tibi virtus hujus in ore viri:
Libertas quanquam pictoribus atque poëtis
Audendi semper quidlibet æqua fuit:
Carmine mentitum nihil hoc liquet esse poëtam;
Mentitus nihil est pictor in arte sua. Joha: Ow:.

Si: Passæus sculp: Lon:.   Compton Holland excud:.

Lord Chancellor Ellesmere

tune of the day; the plaintiffs were non-suited, and our young student was from that day considered to be of great mark and likelihood.[A]

I need hardly ask my reader if he does not hear overtones and echoes from this anecdote in the first part of the trial scene of *The Merchant of Venice*. Shakespeare was probably not familiar with this particular incident where grave injustice might have been done but for the skill and ingenuity of some Portia, as *Amicus Curiae*, "sent for to determine this;" but the atmosphere of this trial and similar ones had permeated the whole system of jurisprudence of his day. He most assuredly was familiar with many such trials, of which this is but a common type, and must have decided that the administration of justice was out of joint with the other members of the body politic and that it was high time to hold a mirror up to nature, as George Bernard Shaw through the same medium has often done for our own day.

The history of Ellesmere, unlike that of the other two members of that great legal triumvirate of Elizabethan England—Edward Coke and Francis Bacon—is one of continuous advancement and influence, step by step, until the ultimate triumph of equity over the common law in 1616, which Shakespeare by a stroke of genius anticipated so dramatically by two decades.

Ellesmere became Attorney General in 1592, and, during the early tenure of this office, he had as his colleague and solicitor Sir Edward Coke, who had already gained public recognition by his tremendous intellect, his profound knowledge of the common law, and his "unexampled arrogance."[B]

Ellesmere's appointment as Lord Keeper of the Great Seal is officially recorded as follows:

> Serenitati sue visum est secum per dimidiatam fere horam colloqui et tunc cum magno sigill graciosissime abire permisit.[C]

In his *Memoirs of the Reign of Queen Elizabeth*, Birch gives an inkling of the intensity of this struggle between law and equity, for Anthony Bacon, brother of Francis Bacon, writing in 1596 to a friend in Venice, says:

> Into whose place, with extraordinary speed, her Majesty hath *ex proprio motu et speciali gratia* advanced Sir Thomas Egerton, with general applause of both court, city, and county, for the reputation he hath of integrity, law, knowledge, and courage.

And Lord Campbell, writing of the same event, says:

> He had the boldness to question and correct the common law judges and their pedantic rules more freely than Lord Keeper Puckering, Lord Keeper Bacon, or any of his predecessors had done, *and after judgment in actions at law he not infrequently granted injunctions against execution, on the ground of fraud in the plaintiff, or some defect in procedure by which justice had been defeated.*[D]

When Elizabeth, of necessity, called Parliament in 1597, Ellesmere by Royal Command summoned the two houses. The following passage of his speech is worth quoting because of its pertinence to our own time as well as to Shakespeare's:

[A] John Lord Campbell, *Lives of The Lord Chancellors*, Vol. II, pp. 329–330.

[B] *Ibid.*, p. 334.

[C] *Ibid.*, p. 336, The Close Roll, 38 Elizabeth (1596).

[D] *Ibid.*, p. 338. The italics are the writer's. See also Thomas Birch, *Memoirs of the Reign of Queen Elizabeth*.

And whereas the number of laws already made are very great, some also of them being obsolete and worn out of use; others idle and vain, serving to no purpose; some again over heavy and too severe for the offense; others too loose and slack for the faults they are to punish, and many of them so full of difficulties to be understood that they cause many controversies; you are therefore to enter into a due consideration of the said laws, and where you find superfluity to prune, where defect to supply, and where ambiguity to explain, that they be not burthensome but profitable to the commonwealth.[A]

Does not this passage shed some very significant light on the chief question of the time, when one considers that it comes in the opening lines of a speech of convocation of Parliament—a speech such as the President would make when addressing his first Congress?

Is it possible that Shakespeare did not realize that the law was inadequate and out of date and that jurisprudence needed to be set right? Is it not reasonable to assume that he read or heard discussed this speech, when at this time he was writing the trial scene of *The Merchant of Venice* and sounding the very problems mentioned by Lord Ellesmere?

16. "Coke treated such reasoning as a quibble"—Ellesmere and Bacon did not.

W. S. Holdsworth in his great work, *A History of English Law,* thus sums up the events that, I contend, must have influenced Shakespeare when he wrote *The Merchant of Venice* for the amusement and enlightenment of Elizabethan England:

[A] Campbell, *Lives* . . . , Vol. II, p. 341.

When two separate and partially competing jurisdictions exist in one state, a conflict between them is sooner or later inevitable. In Henry II's reign there had been such a conflict between the temporal and ecclesiastical jurisdictions. *A similar conflict arose at the beginning of the sixteenth century between the courts of law and equity.[*]*

The nature and occasion of the conflict had been foreshadowed at the end of the fifteenth century. It had become clear that the law could not be modified upon equitable principles, *unless the Chancellor possessed the power of restraining the parties from proceeding at law, or, if they had already done so, from enforcing judgment.[*]* From the time of Henry VI. there are instances of injunctions issued not only against the parties, but also against their counsel. The judges were naturally hostile to a claim to treat them, by means of an injunction, as they were accustomed to treat other courts by means of a prohibition. In Edward IV.'s reign Fairfax asserted that the King's Bench might forbid the parties from resorting to any other jurisdiction, if the case fell within the jurisdiction of the common law courts. In another case of the same reign, Huse and Fairfax declared that if the Chancellor committed the parties for disobedience to an injunction, they would release them by Habeas Corpus. . . . *At the end of Elizabeth's reign the differences became acute.[B,*]*

Holdsworth recounts the climax of the struggle, which may have been influenced to some extent by the public reaction to the play, as follows:

The matter came to a head in the reign of James I.[C] Coke decided in several cases that imprisonment for disobedience to injunctions issued by Chancery was unlawful. In one case, "it was delivered for a general maxim in law, that if any Court of Equity doth intermeddle with any matters properly triable at the common law, or which concern freehold, they are to be prohibited. . . ."[D] So far did Coke

---

[*] The italics are the writer's.

[B] Sir William S. Holdsworth, *A History of English Law,* Vol. I, pp. 459–461.

[C] See also Campbell, *Lives* . . . , Vol. II, pp. 241–245.

[D] *The English Reports,* Vol. 79 (King's Bench Division, Book VIII) , p. 286.

carry his opposition that he even contended that a decree for specific performance was always unjust to the defendant because "it deprived him of his election either to pay damages or to fulfil his promise."[A] The courts of common law saw well enough that their supremacy was at stake. *"If the party against whom judgment was given, might after judgment given against him at common law, draw the matter into the Chancery, it would tend to the subversion of the common law,* for that no man would sue at the common law, but originally begin in Chancery, seeing at the last he might be brought thither."[B]

On behalf of the court of Chancery it was contended that these injunctions did not interfere with the common law. The judgment stood. All that the Chancellor was concerned with was the conduct of the parties to the case in which judgment had been given. The conduct of the parties, it was contended with some force, had never been in issue in the court of common law.[C] This view is justified by cases of the type of *Courtney* v. *Glanvil*.[D] Glanvil had sold to Courtney for £360 a jewel worth £20, and three other jewels for £100. He took a bond for the payment in the name of one Hampton, and then procured an action to be brought on the bond in Hampton's name. Judgment was by consent entered for Hampton, out of court, in the vacation, Glanvil paying all the costs. On appeal this judgment had been upheld by the courts of common law. Against its enforcement an injunction had been issued. Not, as Lord Ellesmere explained in the *Earl of Oxford's Case,* "for any error or defect in the judgment, but for the hard conscience of the party." He pointed out, in the same case, that

by writs of *audita querela* the judges did in some cases "play the chancellors" by reversing a judgment given.[E]

Coke treated such reasoning as a quibble; and he maintained that the jurisdiction claimed by the Chancellor was contrary to two statutes, the Statute of Praemunire of 1354,[F] and a statute of 1403.[G] Lord Ellesmere had little difficulty in showing, from the wording of the Statute of Praemunire, and from its connexion with preceding legislation, that it referred to those who sued in ecclesiastical courts, not to those who sued in the king's courts. It applied to the court of Rome, and to those courts which, though locally within the realm, were, in the exercise of their jurisdiction, subordinate to foreign courts.[H] The statute of 1403 caused more difficulty. It recited that after a judgment in the king's courts, parties were summoned anew sometimes before the king himself, sometimes before the King's Council, and sometimes before the Parliament. It then enacted that after such judgment the parties and their heirs should be in peace, unless the judgment were reversed by attaint or error. There was authority tending to show that the statute applied to proceedings in the court of Chancery.[I] Both in the Doctor and Student[J] and in the Treatise on the Subpoena[K] this view seems to be taken. But Lord Ellesmere argued that it applied only to matters determinable at common law by way of legal proceeding, and not to proceedings in the Chancery as a court of equity. He relied upon the fact that the Chancery was not specifically mentioned in the statute; and he said that, if it were, it is not the judgment which is

---

[A] *Ibid.,* Vol. 81 (King's Bench Division, Book X), p. 540.

* The italics are the writer's.

[B] See also Coke, . . . *a Commentary upon Littleton* . . . , Vol. III, p. 124.

[C] See also Earl of Oxford's Case, *The English Reports,* Vol. 21 (Chancery Book, Book I), pp. 485–489.

[D] See also *The English Reports,* Vol. 79 (King's Bench Division, Book VIII), pp. 294–295. It is said in the *Reports of Cases in Chancery I,* App. 43, "That not one judgment of a hundred is pronounced in court, nor the case so much as heard or understood by the judges, but entered by attornies."

[E] It was urged in the Earl of Oxford's Case, *op. cit.,* p. 486, that, the judgment in that case being based on a statute, no injunction could issue. Ellesmere retorted with much effect that Coke himself in Bonham's case had said (8 Co. Rep. 118) "that the common law will controul Acts of Parliament for when they are against right and reason, repugnant, or impossible to be performed, the common law will controul it. . . ."

[F] *Year Books,* 27 Edward III, St. I, c. 1.

[G] *Ibid.,* 4 Henry IV, c. 23.

[H] John Selden also took this view; see his *Table Talk,* p. 150.

[I] See also Beck vs. Hesill (Henry VI), Cal. ii, *xii.*

[J] See also Bk. i, c. 18.

[K] See also Francis Hargrave, *Collection of Tracts Relative to Law of England,* Vol. I, p. 348.

examined, but the conduct of the parties and the equity of the case.[A]

*James I. referred the matter to Bacon, then Attorney-General, and other counsel, to advise. They advised that there was a strong current of authority since the reign of Henry VII. in favour of the issue of injunctions after judgment, and even after execution;*** that there were cases in which the judges themselves had advised the parties to seek relief in Chancery;[B] and that the practice was not contrary to the statute[C] of 1403. *In accordance with their opinion, James issued on 26 July, 1616, an order in favour of the Chancery.*** It may be that the decision was slightly tinged by political considerations. The common law judges, especially Coke, were already tending to manifest an independence opposed to James's absolutist claims. The Chancellor, as a minister of state, was more favourable to these claims.[D] But, considering the rigidity of the practice of the courts of common law at that period, it cannot be said that the views for which the Chancellor contended were unreasonable.[E]

Lord Chancellor Ellesmere's version of the incidents that preceded the climax to the struggle is given in an instrument endorsed in his own hand from which the following passage is taken:

Prooffes of the proceedinges, the last day of Hillary Terme:

Glanvill, informing the Lord Coke that the Jury wold not finde the bills of Premunire, the Lord Coke sent for the Jury, yet protested he knewe nothing of the matter.

The Jury, for the waightines of the case, desired further tyme and counsill, though at theire owne charge; but both denied, by the Lord Coke affirming that the case was plaine.

The Lord Coke, perceiving the Jury were inclined not to find the bills, they alleadging that they were promised better evidence than the oath of the parties, and that they were not satisfied that the judgement was dulye gotten, being obtained out of Terme, he stood upp and said to them, "Have you not seen copies of the proceedinges in Chancery? Have not Allen and Glanvil made oath for the King that the same are true? Is not a party robbed a good witnes for the King against a theefe, and is there not a judgement in the case?"

At the Jurors' second comeing to the Barre, the Lord Coke said unto them, that yf they wold not find the bills, he wolde comitt them, and said that he wold sitt by it untill the busines were done, and willed them to goe together againe. After which, a Tipstaff attending that Court came into the private room where the Jury were conferring touching those indictments, and told them the Lord Coke was angrye they staid soe long, and bade them feare nothing, the Lord Chancellor was dead.

At the Jurors' third comeing, the Lord Coke caused them to be called by the poll, and perceiving that 17 of the 19 were agreed to return *Ignoramus,* he seemed to be much offended, and then said they had been instructed and tampered withall, and asked Glanvill and Allen to prepare themselves against the next Terme, when he wold have a more sufficient Jury, and evidence given openly at the Barr.

Note, that upon the Lord Coke's threatening wordes one of the Jury formerly agreed with the rest fell from them, saying he found the Bills, Lord Coke said, "I think theis Bills wilbe found anon."

Upon a motion made there that day between Goodwin and Goldsmith concerning a judgment in that Court, the Lord Coke said openly to the lawyers, "Take it for a warning, whosoever shall putt his hand to a bill in any English Court after a judgement at lawe, wee will foreclose hym for ever speaking more in this Court. I give you a faire warning to preserve you from a greater mischief. Some must be made example, and on whome it lighteth it will fall heavy. Wee must looke about us, or the common law of England wilbe overthrowne."

[A] See also Earl of Oxford's Case, *op. cit.*, paragraphs 10, 15. But the tract in the Office of the Chancellor 49, 50, and another tract, called "A Treatise on the Privileges and Prerogatives of the High Court of Chancery," take the other view.

[*] The italics are the writer's.

[B] See also *Reports of Cases in Chancery I*, App. 2, p. 12; cp. Smith vs. Crokew, Star Chamber Cases (C.S.), p. 38.

[C] *Ibid.*, p. 14–25.

[D] Ellesmere's bias in favor of high prerogative views comes out strongly in his treatment of James Whitelock, *Liber Famelicus* (C.S.), pp. 33–41.

[E] Holdsworth, *A History* . . . , Vol. I, pp. 461–463.

And said further, that the Judges shold have little to doe at the assizes by reason the light of the lawe was lyke to be obscured, and therefore, since the said case then moved was after judgment, he willed the party to preferr an indictment of praemunire.

> Note, the Lord Coke said the Judges of that Court were the superintendents of the realm. (Unpublished MS. in possession of Lord Francis Egerton.) ᴬ

I now quote from Cary whose private *Reports* have become a part of the countless number of reported cases that *are* the common law of England. Cary realized the great importance of this case and in his *Reports* quoted the full transcript of the commission appointed by James I to determine this matter. This transcript signed by Francis Bacon and Henry Yelverton is as follows:

[115] THE KING'S ORDER AND DECREE IN CHANCERY, FOR A RULE TO BE OBSERVED BY THE CHANCELLOR IN THAT COURT; EXEMPLIFIED AND ENROLLED FOR A PERPETUAL RECORD THERE. ANNO 1616.

James by the Grace of God, &c. Whereas our Right Trusty and Well-beloved Sir Francis Bacon, Knight, our Counsellor and Attorney-General, received a letter from our Chancellor of England, dated the 19th of March, An. Dom. 1615. Written by our express Commandment, directing him, and requiring him, and the rest of our learned Counsel, to peruse such precedents as should be produced unto them, from time of King Henry the Seventh, and since, of complaints made in the Chancery, there to be relieved according to equity and conscience, after judgments in the Courts of the Common Laws, in cases wherein the Judges of the common law could not relieve them: And thereupon to certify us of the truth of that they shall find, and of their opinions concerning the (116) same, which letter followeth in these words:—

Master Attorney, his Majesty being informed that there may be precedents in the Court of Chancery, in the time of King Henry 7, and continually since, that such as complained there to be relieved according to equity and conscience, after judgments in the Courts of the Common Law, in cases where the Judges of the common law could not relieve them (being bound by their oath, to observe the strict rules of the law) is willing to understand, whether there be such precedents as he is informed of: And therefore hath commanded me to let you know, that his will and pleasure is, that you call to assist you his Majesty's Serjeants and Solicitor, and to peruse such precedents of this kind, as shall be produced unto you; and thereupon to certify his Majesty of the truth of that you shall find, and of your opinions concerning the same; and for your better directions therein, I have sent you here enclosed a note in writing delivered unto me, mentioning some such precedents in King Henry the Seventh's time and since. And I am told (117) that there be the like in former times; his Majesty expecteth your proceeding in this with as much speed as conveniently you may: And so I rest,—Your very assured loving Friend,

T. ELLESMERE. *Canc.*

At York House, 19th Martii, 1615.

And whereas our Attorney-General, and the rest of our learned counsel did there-upon return unto us their certificate, subscribed with all their hands, according to our commandment and direction given them by the said letter, which certificate followeth in these words:—

According to your Majesty's commandment, we have advisedly considered of the note delivered unto us, of precedents of complaining and proceeding in Chancery after judgments in Common Law:* and also have seen and perused the originals, out of which the same note was abstracted: upon all which we do find, and observe the points following:—

1. We find that the same note is fully verified, and maintained by the originals.

(118) 2. *We find that there hath been a strong current of practice of proceeding in Chancery after judgment, and many times after execution, continued from the beginning of Henry the Seventh's reign, unto the time of the Lord Chancellor that now is,* both in the reigns (separatim) of the several Kings, and in the times of the several Chancellors, whereof divers were great*

ᴬ Campbell, *Lives* . . . , Vol. II, pp. 387–389.

* The italics are the writer's.

learned men in the law: it being in cases where there is no remedy for the subject, by the strict course of the common law, unto which the Judges are sworn.

3. We find that these proceedings in Chancery, hath been after judgments, in actions of several natures, as well real as personal.

4. We find it hath been after judgments in your Majesty's several Courts, the King's Bench, Common Pleas, Justice in Oyer, &c.

5. We find it hath been after judgments obtained upon verdict, demurrers, and where writs of error have been brought.

6. We find in many of the cases, that the judgments are expressly mentioned in the bills in the Chancery themselves (119) to have been given, and relief prayed thereupon sometimes for stay of execution, sometimes after execution, of which kind we find a great number in King Henry the Seventh's time.

7. We find the matters in equity laid in such bills in most of the cases, to have been matter precedent before the judgments, and not matter of agreement after.

8. We find in the said cases, not only the bill preferred, but motions, orders, injunctions, and decrees thereupon, for the discharging and releasing of the judgments, or abiding the possession thereupon obtained, and sometimes for the mean profits, and the release of the costs, &c.

9. We find in some of the cases in this very point, that judgment hath been given, hath been stood upon by the defendants, and alledged by them by way of demurrer, and over-ruled.

10. We find that the Judges themselves, in their own Courts, when there appeared unto them matter of equity, because they by their oath and office could not stay the judgments, except it be for some small time, have directed the par- (120) ties to seek relief in Chancery.

11. We find that this hath not only been in the times of the several Chancellors, but by the Judges themselves, and that without difficulty, when they sat in Chancery, in the vacancy or absence of the Chancellor.

12. We find the hands of sundry principal Counsellors at Law, whereof divers of them are now Judges, and some in chief place, in bills of this kind.

13. Lastly, here were offered to have been shewed

unto us many other precedents, whereof we heard some read, and found them to be of like nature with those contained in the note.

FRANCIS BACON,
RANDELL CREW,
HENRY MOUNTAGUE,
HENRY YELVERTON.

And whereas also our said Attorney received one other letter from our said Chancellor, with a case there inclosed, written likewise by our express commandment, dated the 27th of March, 1616, directing and requiring him, and the rest of our learned counsel, together with the attorney of our dear Son the Prince, to confer together upon the said cause, and to consider advisedly of all the parts thereof; and thereupon to peruse (121) all the statutes of *praemunire,* or provisoes, and all other statutes as they shall conceive to be necessary to be considered of, for the resolving the question propounded in that case; and thereupon to report unto us their opinions in writing concerning the same; which letter and case there inclosed follow in these words:—

Master Attorney, His Majesty hath perused this case inclosed, and hath commanded me to send it to you; and his will and pleasure is, that you call unto you Mr. Serjeant Mountague, Mr. Serjeant Crew, Mr. Solicitor, and Mr. Walter, the Prince's Attorney and that you confer together thereupon, and consider advisedly and deliberately of all the parts thereof; and thereupon to peruse all the statutes of *praemunire* or provisoes, and all other such statutes as you shall conceive to be necessary to be considered of, for the resolving the question propounded in this case; this His Majesty would have be done with mature deliberation, and yet with as much speed as conveniently you can; and when you have sufficiently informed (122) yourselves therein, then to report to him your opinions in writing; and so I commit you to God, and rest, —Your very loving friend,

T. ELLESMERE, *Canc.*
At York House, the 27th of March, 1616.

A hath judgment and execution in the King's Bench or Common Pleas, against B in an action for debt of one thousand pounds. And in an *ejectione firmae,* of the manor of D, B complains in the Chancery to be relieved against those judgments according to conscience and equity, allowing the judgments to be lawful and good by the rigour and strict rules of the common laws;[A] and the matters in conscience and equity, such as the Judges of the common law (being no Judges in equity, but bound by their oaths to do the law)[B] cannot give any remedy or relief for the same, either by error or attaint, or by any other means. *Questio.* Whether the Chancery may relieve B in this or such like cases, or else leave him utterly remediless and undone; and if the Chancery be restrained by any statute of *praemunire,* (123) &c. Then by what statute, or by what words in any statute, is the Chancery so restrained, and conscience and equity banished, excluded and damned?[C]

And whereas, according to our said commandment, our said learned Counsel, and the Attorney of our dear Son the Prince, returned unto us a certificate of their opinions upon the said statutes, under all their several hands, concerning the same case, which certificate followeth in these words:—

According to your Majesty's commandment, we have deliberately advised of the case sent unto us by the Lord Chancellor, and of the statutes, as well those of *praemunire* as others, as far as we take it may concern the case; and for our better information therein, we have thought fit to send for and peruse the original records themselves, remaining in the Tower of London, of those statutes not only appearing upon the roll of Parliament, with the King's answers, which is the warrant to the roll of Parliament.

We have also taken into consideration, as well book laws, as divers other acts[D] of Parliament, which may give light (124) unto the statutes, whereupon the question properly grows, together with such ancient records and precedents[E] as we could find, as well as those which maintain the authority of the Chancery, as those which seem to impeach the same; and upon the whole matter, we are all of opinion, that the Chancery may give relief to the case in question;[F] and that no

statute of praemunire, &c., or other statute restrains the same.

And because we know not what use your Majesty will be pleased to make of this our opinion,[G] either for the time present or future, we are willing to give some reasons of the same, not thinking fit to trouble your Majesty with all those things whereupon we have grounded ourselves, selecting out some principal things, which moved us to be of this opinion, to the end this same may be a fuller object of your Majesty's princely judgment, whereunto we always submit ourselves.

And first, we must lay for a sure foundation that which was contained in our former certificate, concerning the continual practice, by the space now of six score years, in the times of King (125) Henry the 7th, King Henry the 8th, King Edward the 6th, Queen Mary, and Queen Elizabeth, of this authority; and that in the time when the same authority was managed, not only by the Bishops, which might be thought less skilful, or less affectionate towards the laws of the land, but also divers great lawyers, which could not but know and honour the law, as the means of their advancement, Sir Thomas More, and the Lord Audly, the Lord Rich, Sir Nicholas Bacon, Sir Thomas Bromley, and Sir John Puckering; and further that most of the late Judges of the kingdom, either as Judges when they sat in Chancery by commission, or as counsellors at law, when they set their hands to bills, have by their judgment and counsel upheld the same authority; and therefore, forasmuch as it is a true ground, that *optimus legum interpres consuetudo,* especially when the practice or custom passeth not amongst vulgar persons, but amongst the most high and scient magistrates of the kingdom; and when also the practising of the same should lie under so heavy a pain as the *praemunire;* this is to us a principal and implicit satisfac- (126) tion; and those statutes ought not to be construed to extend to this case; and this of itself we know is of far more force to move Your Majesty than any opinion of ours, because Kings are fittest to inform Kings and Chancellors to teach Chancellors, and Judges to teach Judges; but further, out of our own science and profession,

---

[A] ". . . this strict court of Venice

Must needs give sentence 'gainst the merchant there." (205)

[B] ". . . the law allows it, and the court awards it." (303)

[C] This hypothetical case is, in principle, identical with Antonio's case.

[D] "Thyself shalt see the act. . . ." (314)

[E] " 'Twill be recorded for a precedent. . . ." (220)

[F] This is the same relief which the writer contends Antonio received.

[G] ". . . he is furnished with my opinion. . . ." (159)

we have thought fit to add these further reasons and proofs very briefly, because in case of so ancient a possession of jurisdiction, we hold it not fit to amplify.[A]

Now follow the fifteen technical reasons that were the basis for the decision of the committee appointed by the King. These I have omitted, and now we proceed directly to the conclusion reached by the committee and the official pronouncement of Francis Bacon and Henry Yelverton *"Per Ipsum Regum"*:

There be divers other things of weight which we have seen and considered of, whereupon we have grounded our opinion, but we go no further upon that we have seen.

But because matters of precedents are greatly considerable in this case, and that we have been attended by the clerks of the Chancery, with the precedents of that Court, and have not been yet attended by any officer of the King's Bench, with any precedents of judgments, if it shall please your Majesty, a faithful report of them, as we have done of the other; all which, &c.

> FRANCIS BACON,
> RANDALL CREW,
> JOHN WALTER,
> HENRY MONTAGUE,
> HENRY YELVERTON.

Now, forasmuch as *mercy and justice be the true supports of our Royal Throne, and that it properly belongeth to us, in our princely office,** to take care and provide, that our subjects have equal and indifferent justice ministered (134) to them; and that where their case deserveth to be relieved in course of equity, by suit in our Court of Chancery, they should not be abandoned, and exposed to perish under the rigour and extremity of our laws; We, in our princely judgment, having well weighed, and with mature deliberation considered of the said several reports of our learned Counsel, and of all parts of them, do approve, ratify, and confirm, as well the practice of our

Court of Chancery, expressed in the first certificate, as their opinions for the law upon the statutes mentioned in their latter certificate, the same having relation to the case sent them by our said Chancellor; and do will and command, that our Chancellor, or Keeper of the Great Seal, for the time being, shall not hereafter desist unto our subjects upon their several complaints (now or hereafter to be made) such relief in equity (notwithstanding any former proceedings at common law against them) as shall stand with true merits and justice of their cases, and with the former ancient and continued practice and proceeding of our Chancery; and for that it apper- (135) taineth to our princely care and office only to judge over all our Judges, and to discern and determine such differences as at any time may or shall arise between our several Courts, touching the jurisdiction, and the same to settle and decide as we in our princely wisdom shall find to stand most with our honour, and the example of our Royal Progenitors, in the best times, and the general weal and good of our people, for which we are to answer unto God, who hath placed us over them: our will and pleasure is, that our whole proceedings herein, by the decrees formerly set down, be enrolled in our Court of Chancery, there to remain of record, for the better extinguishing of the like questions or differences that may arise in future times.

> *Per Ipsum Regum* [sic]
> FRANCIS BACON,
> HENRY YELVERTON.

Decimo octavo Julii, Anno 14 R. Regis, &c.[B]

Thus is the concluding chapter written by a contemporary of Shakespeare—a man his senior by two years—who had lived to its fullest the life of an Elizabethan. To illustrate my point that the trial scene of *The Merchant of Venice* may have had a profound effect upon the shaping of jurisprudence at this time, I merely quote a few lines of Portia's famous equitable plea for comparison with the opening lines of Sir Francis Bacon's official act *"Per Ipsum Regum."* [sic]

[A] *The English Reports,* Vol. 21, pp. 61–63.
* The italics are the writer's.

[B] *Ibid.,* p. 65.

The quality of mercy is not strain'd,

.   .   .   .

It becomes the Throned monarch better than his
    crown;

.   .   .   .

It is enthroned in the hearts of kings,

.   .   .   .

And earthly power doth then show likest God's
When mercy seasons justice. [184 *et seq.*]

Now, forasmuch as mercy and justice be the
true supports of our Royal Throne, and that it
properly belongeth to us, in our princely office,
to take care and provide, that our subjects have
equal and indifferent justice ministered to
them. . . .[A]

Here once more is an echo from Shakespeare's drama, caught and made permanent in the official records of this drama of
reality upon which, I contend, the play
had its effect.

James I issued a proclamation that no
new buildings should be erected in London for a definite time and that no starch
should be made from wheat flour. Justice
Coke denied this right of the Sovereign on
the grounds that Parliament and not the
King was the source of statutory law. Lord
Ellesmere, the Chancellor, supported the
King in his contention that he, the King,
could make certain limited proclamations
which were enforceable and binding at
common law.

Ellesmere, having in mind the flexibility
of equity and the elasticity of its writs, is
reported to have said, in behalf of the
King's prerogative, before the council
where all the judges had been summoned
to decide the matter:

> . . . that every precedent must have a first com-
> mencement, and that he would advise the Judges
> to maintain the power and prerogative of the
> King; and in cases in which there is no authority
> and precedent, to leave it to the King to order it

according to his wisdom and the good of his subjects, for otherwise the King *would be no more
than the Duke of Venice*.[B]

The phrase, "would be no more than
the Duke of Venice," would seem to indicate that Lord Ellesmere was at least aware
of the trial scene in *The Merchant of
Venice* when considered in relation to the
opening stage directions.

If Justice Coke prevailed, the King
would have no power to enforce his proclamation; and, in the opinion of Lord
Ellesmere, the King would have no more
power to enforce his own proclamations
than the Duke of Venice, in the trial scene,
would have to uphold his own judgment
in favor of Shylocke.

17. "Let me have judgement and the Jew his will."

In the King vs. Briggs (2 Buls 295), Sir
Francis Bacon, when acting as Attorney
General, entered a confession of judgment
which Lord Chief Justice Coke at first refused to allow because of the novelty of
the procedure in common law, where only
confessions of fact and not law were considered (10 James I, 1613).[C]

18. "How shalt thou hope for mercy, rendering none?"

The earliest extant work on the maxims of
law and equity was written and published
by Sir Francis Bacon about the time that is

[A] *Ibid.*

[B] Campbell, *Lives* . . . , Vol. II, p. 385. The italics
are the writer's.
[C] *The English Reports*, Vol. 21, p. 295.

now designated as the fourth period of Shakespeare's dramatic production.

One of the best and earliest legal interpretations of the maxim, "He who seeks equity must do equity," is used in a quotation by Pomeroy:

> The court of equity refuses its aid to give to the plaintiff what the law would give him if the courts of common law had jurisdiction to enforce it, without imposing upon him conditions which the court considers he ought to comply with, although the subject of the condition should be one which the court would not otherwise enforce.[A]
>
> This maxim expresses a cardinal principle and is one of the oldest in equity jurisprudence.[B]

These maxims express the cardinal principles on which equity has developed and reach so far back into antiquity that we have them without any definite authority for their source and origin. I shall quote a few of the fourteen maxims which are the foundation stones of equity: "Equality is equity,"[C] "Equity regards . . . that as done which ought to be done,"[D] "Equity will not suffer a wrong without a remedy,"[E] "Equity regards the spirit and not the letter, the intent and not the form, the substance rather than the circumstance,"[F] "Equity imputes an intention to perform an obligation,"[G] "Equity tries to do justice and not by halves."

19. "Equity abhors a forfeiture."

The case of Wiseman vs. Roper arose from an agreement to sell lands, by a contracting party who did not have possession of the lands but only the possibility of inheriting them. When he did inherit the lands he was sued at common law. The only remedy for the plaintiff was money damages for whatever he may have lost by failure to obtain the land he sought to purchase, for there was no common law form of action for the acquisition of land not yet in the possession of the grantor, just as there was no relief for Antonio on the bond at common law. There was a writ or form of action which Shylocke could and did avail himself of, but there was no fair and reasonable defense thereto at common law. The plaintiff in Wiseman vs. Roper who in equity and good conscience was entitled to the property, as Shylocke was not, went to equity for affirmative aid to prevent the forfeiture of his contract, just as Antonio sought the protection of equity to relieve him of the disastrous results of a forfeiture. In Wiseman's case, as in Antonio's, the Chancellor was equal to the occasion and master of the situation; and in decreeing what was equitable in Wiseman's case, he says:

> This Court do find warranted the Precedents and constant Practice of this Court, where such Agreements have been made, upon which the Party can only recover Damages at Law [as the forfeiture] for this Court to decree the Thing in specie [not allow the forfeiture], wherein this Court doth not bind the Interest of the Lands, but inforce the party to perform his own agreement. . . .[H]

Thus, the Chancellor brought about the true enforcement of the contract according to the intent of the parties without violating any principles of equity in so doing.

[A] J. N. Pomeroy, *A Treatise on Equity Jurisprudence*, Ch. I, Sect. III, paragraph 385.

[B] *Corpus Juris*, Vol. 21, pp. 172–173.

[C] Pomeroy, *op. cit.*, Sect. V, paragraphs 405–412.

[D] *Ibid.*, Sect. I, paragraphs 364–377.

[E] *Ibid.*, Sect. X, paragraphs 423–424.

[F] *Ibid.*, Sect. II, paragraphs 378–384.

[G] *Ibid.*, Sect. IX, paragraphs 420–422.

[H] *The English Reports*, Vol. 21, p. 537.

20. "Upon my power I may dismiss this Court. . . ."

It was not uncommon in the reign of Elizabeth for the court to continue a case until the following day or for a reasonable time to suit the convenience of the court or the litigants. I have selected the following case which was tried a few years after her reign as an example of this practice:

In a case moved by Mr. Chamberlain where the Lord Chancellor had referred the matter to be tried at common law, touching remainder on the lease, whether good in law or no, and the judges have given judgment on the case, in another point, in the King's Bench, so as the Lord Chancellor remains still uncertain of that point, called the judges into Exchequer Chamber.[A] [1 James I, 1604]

21. "Bellario, . . . , Whom I have sent for to determine this,". . . .

Friend of the court (*Amicus Curiae*) was and is a term applied to one who, of his own volition or at the request of the court as in the case of Shakespeare's trial judge, advises the court on an unusual "cause in controversy" and thereby helps direct the meandering flow of the decisional current to the great ocean of the common law.

Lord Chief Justice Coke makes the following statement about *Amicus Curiae:*

This custom cannot be traced to its origin but is immemorial in the English law. It is recognized in the Year Books, and it was enacted in 4 Hen. IV (1403) that any stranger as *"Amicus Curiae"* might move the court, etc. The custom

included *instructing, warning,* and *moving* the court. The information so communicated may extend to any matter of which the court takes judicial cognizance;[B]

I am confident that, in the light of the law as it was then and as it is now, Shakespeare's judge did not contemplate an unprecedented action when he said:

Upon my power I may dismiss this Court,
Unless Bellario, a learned doctor,
Whom I have sent for to determine this,
Come here to-day. [104]

22. Sir Francis Bacon.

The introduction of Bacon as *Amicus Curiae* is not intended to aid and abet the advocates of the Baconian authorship of the plays. It should be clear from the tenor of this study that the writer is convinced of the identity of the "Man of Stratford" with the author of the Shakespearean canon. But, on the other hand, the introduction of Bacon as *Amicus Curiae,* who solves the conflict between "Law" and "Equity," is intended to suggest the actual fact that it was Bacon's destiny as a legal authority to solve the actual conflict which Portia solves in the play.

He who was destined to rise so high and fall so low was born just three years before Shakespeare. The son of the Lord Keeper of the King's Seal and the nephew of the powerful Lord Burghley was christened Francis Bacon in the month of February, 1561. When only twelve years of age he matriculated at Trinity College, Cambridge, and after pursuing his studies most

[A] *Reports of Cases in Chancery I,* p. 25.

[B] Coke, *Reports* . . . , Vol. VIII, p. 15, "The Prince's Case."

Sir Francis Bacon

diligently for three years he entered Gray's Inn, where his father and grandfather before him had studied law and where other descendants were also destined to follow the Bacon tradition.

The great favorite of the Queen and patron of the stage at this time was the Earl of Essex, whose patronage Bacon sought as did Shakespeare and many of his contemporaries. Bacon won the favor of Essex, but this rare combination of circumstances was not sufficient to overcome the antipathy which the Queen bore him because of an act in his early career. He, as a member of the House of Commons, became the leader of the opposition to a bill to increase taxes which was instituted in the House of Lords. Bacon did not oppose the bill on its merits but because of its origin in the House of Lords which he thought was a great threat to the dearly won power of the House of Commons. This bill was sponsored by the Queen herself, a most significant fact that was not made known to Bacon before his attack upon it.

Elizabeth never forgave him, and Essex at the height of his influence could not procure for Bacon a public office, and, therefore, his only official contact with the state in his early life was that most unpleasant experience of imprisonment in the Fleet for debt.

To prevent a repetition of this experience, he entered the public practice of law and in 1594 took an active part in the trial of Chudleigh's Case which established the rule against perpetuities limiting the duration of trusts similar to the one created by Shylocke.

He became eminently successful in the practice of law and in the writing of philosophical treatises.

His power as a philosopher perhaps caused him to be a failure as a statesman, for the thinker influences future thought more powerfully than he can hope to impress contemporaries.[A]

Bacon had one contemporary who was also a philosophic thinker, and, whether they be contemporaries or of different ages, one seer will influence another. In this instance the mental seeds of Bacon fell upon fertile ground in the mind of the country boy from Stratford and bore fruit in the form of the trial scene of *The Merchant of Venice*. As is often the case there was a crossing of the species when Bacon, as he undoubtedly must have done, saw this scene enacted before his eyes and realized the incongruity of the conflicting principles of law and equity placed in such a beautiful juxtaposition. Thus, when the wheel had gone full turn, it was Bacon who, a few years later, echoed the spirit of the last part of this scene in his report to Elizabeth's successor in which he cast his vote in favor of Ellesmere and equity and against Justice Coke and the *strictum jus*. It was this additional weight in the balance in favor of equity that ended the struggle of several centuries.[B]

23. Bill for "Injunction to stay suit at common law."

It is quite evident from the *Year Books* and earliest *Chancery Reports* that the Chancellors were not limited by strict formality of pleading, as were the common law judges, and often heard a plea on a bill that was ineffectual at common law.

[A] The Earl of Birkenhead, *op. cit.*, p. 12.

[B] *Ibid.* The writer acknowledges his indebtedness for the general outline of this note and many of the facts contained therein.

Si en cest court il n'est requisiti que le bill soit tout en certain solon que le solemnity del comen ley. [Pasmore vs. Ford, 23 Elizabeth (1581) ; Choyce Cases 147.][A]

The reports of Cary and Choyce, as well as the other reports of the sixteenth century, are filled with innumerable cases where a litigant brought a suit at common law in the Court of Common Pleas or in the King's Bench, and the defendant appeared in answer to the writ. These cases were allowed to "proceed to judgment" (240) and then the defendant, if the judgment was against him, would immediately go into the Court of Chancery and inform the Chancellor of his predicament. If his cause was worthy, the Chancellor would allow a temporary injunction which, in effect, prohibited the successful litigant in the court of law from exercising the rights under his judgment. This practice had become so common by the end of the sixteenth century that both the Chancellor and the judges at common law realized that it could not long continue without some definite settlement of the conflict. The following is one of the numerous cases on this point reported by Cary:

KNIGHT *v.* HARTWELL

Injunction to stay suit at common law.—The defendant did tender an assurance to the father to be sealed, who being old and blind, desired time to confer with his friends; the plaintant, upon request, sealed the assurance, and his father afterwards sent word to the defendant he was willing to seal it, but the defendant answered, he did not pass whether he did or no, because he had but an estate for his life, and the defendant had his bond to enjoy it during his life, which he did according; and yet nevertheless the defendant put the bond in suit

upon his father's said refusal, but [he was] stayed by injunction. . . .[B] [1578–79]

24. The Court of Exchequer Chamber.[C]

From the fourteenth century to the middle of the sixteenth century, the Exchequer Chamber heard only what today would be tax-appeal cases; but after 1550 it claimed and exercised, as the result of a logical conceit, namely, that the income of the realm was affected adversely by any lawsuit, appellate jurisdiction in actions at common law, and suits in chancery.[D]

In the year 1585, by the statute of 27 Elizabeth, a second Court of Exchequer Chamber was created with appellate jurisdiction over the Court of King's Bench and the Court of Chancery. This Court of Exchequer Chamber consisted of the judges of the Common Pleas and the Barons of the Exchequer, any six of whom might render judgment. From such judgments there was a further appeal to Parliament.[E]

25. ". . . I will seal unto this bond."

It was settled law in the reign of Edward I that certain instruments must be under seal before they could be used as the basis of a cause of action at law:

Non solum sufficiet scriptura nisi sigilli munimine stipulantes roboetur cum testiminio fide

---

[A] *The English Reports,* Vol. 21, p. 87, has an English translation.

[B] *Ibid.,* p. 56.
[C] See also note 54.
[D] The writer is indebted to Morgan, *op. cit.,* Ch. I, for the facts contained herein.
[E] *Ibid.*

dignorum praesintium. [*Year Books*, 30 Edward I (R.S.), p. 158.]A

No doubt Pollock and Maitland are correct when they attribute the historical significance of the sealing of an instrument to the fact that it was a most solemn act that could not be done by the common people but only by those who possessed a *signum* with which to impress their seal upon an instrument. These authorities say that this practice is

. . . no product of the ancient folk-law. The 'act and deed' that is chosen is one that in the past has been possible only to men of the highest rank.B

But there was another historical reason which was of more importance, namely, that the sealing of an instrument was irrebuttable proof that the one whose seal was attached thereto was bound to the party named in the instrument. This is shown by an early case very closely in point with Shylocke vs. Antonio. Note this language of Spigurnel, Judge, in the *Eyre of Kent*, Vol. II, p. 10:

If a man by a writing confesses himself indebted to us, and the writing goes on to say "and for further security I procure such an one who binds himself," and this latter affixes his seal to the writing, how can you argue that he does not say the same thing as the other man says? He affirms it by the fact of affixing his seal; and so you must answer to the deed.C

Could we not substitute the names of Bassanio, Antonio, and Shylocke in this case and have Antonio bound to Shylocke as surety on Bassanio's bond? And would not Antonio be liable on the bond at common law, even though he got nothing for his promise in the form of *quid pro quo,* for it was Bassanio who got the 3,000 ducats?

Chief Justice Holmes in his work, *The Common Law,* reaches the conclusion that by the end of the fifteenth century a covenant or contract under seal was "no longer a promise well proved," but was then "a promise of a distinct nature, for which a distinct form of action came to be provided."D

In later days, when the doctrine of consideration had come to be the most distinctive feature of the English law of contract, these contracts under seal were thought to be brought into line with the general rule requiring consideration, by saying that the seal imports a consideration, and that the parties were therefore bound. This view that a seal imports a consideration was put forward as early as 1566. . . .E

SHARINGTON *v.* STROTTON

Where it is by deed [instrument under seal] the cause or consideration is not enquirable, nor is it to be weighed [one pound of flesh for 3,000 ducats], but the party ought to answer to the deed, and if he confesses it to be his deed ["do you confess the bond?"], he shall be bound, for every deed imports in itself a consideration. . . . And in an action of debt upon an obligation, the consideration upon which the party made the deed is not to be enquired, for it is sufficient to say that it was his will to make the deed. [Plowden, *Reports,* p. 309 (1566).]F

An interesting backstage view of the workings of the minds of pre-Elizabethan lawyers on the *quid pro quo* in a contract is shown by two cases, the facts of which are

A "*Les Reports des Cases en Ley Que furent argues in temps Du Roy Edward le Premier.*"
B Sir Frederick Pollock and Frederic William Maitland, *The History of English Law,* Vol. II, p. 223.
C Holdsworth, *A History* . . . , Vol. III, p. 417, note 4.
D Oliver Wendell Holmes, *The Common Law,* pp. 272–273.
E Holdsworth, *A History* . . . , Vol. III, p. 419.
F *Ibid.,* note 5.

identical. These cases were tried in the reign of Henry VI, with an intervening span of exactly thirty years. In each, "A" brought an action of debt against "B," in which he alleged in a petition that "B" had promised him a certain sum of money if he, "A," would marry "B's" daughter; that he, "A," had performed his part of the contract by marrying "B's" daughter and that "B" had refused and continued to refuse to pay him, "A," the sum of money agreed upon. In both of these cases the entire argument for the defendant, "B," was that there was no consideration or *quid pro quo*, for the marrying of one's daughter was not an act that could be considered of benefit to the defendant. And if the defendant had not received some benefit from this action of the plaintiff, for which the plaintiff in turn had sacrificed something of value, there was no common law consideration unless, of course, the instrument be sealed. In the first case[A] the court decided that "A" could not collect the money "B" had promised because the contract was not sealed, nor was "A's" act sufficient consideration to support "B's" promise.

In the second case,[B] the court, for social, economic, and other reasons, reached the conclusion that "A" had done a service for "B" (the record does not disclose whether the daughter was introduced into evidence in either case) and, therefore, at law, was entitled to the sum promised for his services.[C]

[A] *Year Books*, 7 Henry VI, Michaelis Term, p. 1, plea 3.

[B] *Ibid.*, 37 Henry VI, Michaelis Term, p. 13, plea 18.

[C] See Holdsworth, *A History* . . . , Vol. III, pp. 419 *et seq.*, for additional information.

26. "Go with me to a notary."

The English notary is of ecclesiastical origin and was of very little importance until the fifteenth and sixteenth centuries when not only ecclesiastics but also laymen became notaries. Thus, the notary in the time of Shakespeare had become a common and rather important figure in the business affairs of Elizabethan merchants. His increased importance was due to the great awakening of English trade and commerce. Therefore, the notary in England assumed some of the importance of his continental brother, for it was he who was employed, because of his skill and the dignity of his office, to prepare certain documents and contracts, such as charter parties, bonds, negotiable instruments, insurance contracts, leases, and other important documents.

One of the earliest instances of the activity of a notary is recorded in the *Parliamentary Rolls of England* (R.P.), Vol. III, p. 416, in which it is recorded that notaries were the ones entrusted with the solemn duty of giving Richard II notice of his deposition and to receive his resignation (1399).

When, in the latter part of the sixteenth century, the demand for the services of notaries exceeded their ability to serve, the members of the Scriveners Company were permitted, by charter from the King, to act in that capacity, and even today all notaries are members of this modern counterpart of the ancient guild.

As a man who could earn and spend a thousand pounds in a year, Shakespeare was certainly familiar with commercial transactions, and knew the respect that would be shown an instrument acknowledged before a notary and the evidentiary weight that it would have in a court of common law.

27. The court having jurisdiction of "the cause."

There was no doubt, after the ruling in the Exchequer Chamber in the case cited in note 25, that the proper place to bring a suit on a bond under seal was in the Court of Common Pleas or the Court of King's Bench, both of which were courts of common law.[A]

Had this bond not been sealed, Shylocke might have been forced to bring his suit in the Court of Admiralty,[B] which at this time was of great importance. This Court of Admiralty, because of the increasing amount of commerce and because of its much wider jurisdiction since the common law courts had failed to limit its jurisdiction to cases arising *super altum mare,* was an active rival of the great common law courts of Common Pleas and King's Bench.

28. The evidentiary effect of a sealed instrument.

Because of the fact that a sealed instrument was considered irrebuttable evidence of the obligation of the maker to the party named therein, the only procedure necessary for the holder of such an instrument was to obtain the proper writ, file the proper petition, and present himself and his instrument in court and therewith confront the defendant.

29. ". . . whether you'll admit him."

The blunt and brutal truth is that the earliest lawsuits were fights, and no lawyers were allowed to participate therein because it was a case of might making right, and a litigant was forced to use his own might to prove his own right.

Bracton describes the professional "champion" in his reports of the cases of "trial by battle"[C] as early as 1220, so the pugnacious lawyer has a long pedigree. This calling, however, was not popular and as the "trial by battle" disappeared, so did the "champion" and in his place developed the *serviens ad legem* and his clerk or *responsalis,* all of whom were under official license of the King.

There was a marked increase in the use of law to settle individual disputes at the close of the thirteenth century because of the changing condition in the social and economic state of England and, therefore, an increasing scarcity of these *serviens ad legem* as shown by the parliamentary roll of the year 1292. This scarcity of servants of the law was so marked at this time that the itinerant justices and the justices of the Common Pleas and the King's Bench sent out their clerks to search for those who possessed a license from the King to practice law.

To Shakespeare and his contemporaries, the solicitors and attorneys were a very real class, although there was an early distinction between the two, and the attorney was considered of higher rank. In 1559, the solicitors are not mentioned along with the attorneys in the orders of the Inns of

---

[A] See note 2.
[B] See note 10.

[C] Henry de Bracton, *Notebook,* Vol. II, case 116.

Court,[A] but the fact that they were so mentioned in the orders of the judges and the Privy Council of 1574 concerns us, for to be included in such an order was to be eligible to practice before the courts of the realm. By the last decade of the sixteenth century, it is quite evident that this question of the eligibility of solicitors to practice in the courts was settled. This was quite an important question which was much discussed by the Elizabethans and one which Shakespeare had in mind when he had Nerissa say of the young lawyer sent by Bellario:

He attendeth here hard by,
To know your answer, whether you'll admit him.
[146]

This question was settled by the following order that appeared in the year in which the play was written:

If any hereafter admitted in court, practise as Attorney or Solicitor, they to be dismissed and expulsed out of their Houses thereupon; except the persons that shall be Solicitors shall also use the exercising of learning and mooting in the House, and so be allowed by the Bench.[B]

30. The "cause in controversy."

This is a perfect example of the proper use of a technical legal term which shows beyond doubt that the dramatist had more than a superficial knowledge of legal phraseology.

This term is now of more significance to citizens of the United States than to Shakespeare's countrymen, for, since the time of Chief Justice Marshall, it has been the custom of the United States Supreme Court to hear only a "cause in controversy." (156) The adherence to this custom has prevented this tribunal from determining the constitutionality of an act of Congress by a decision upon a fictitious lawsuit or hypothetical question. We in America must await the decision as to the constitutionality of a law until some individual citizen appeals a "cause in controversy" to the court of last resort.

31. ". . . we turned o'er many books together. . . ."

This proves that Shakespeare knew well the method of the lawyer and the hours of scholarly research required to find "precedents" and authorities in support of his client's "cause."[C]

32. ". . . he is furnished with my opinion. . . ."

This is the proper use of the term, for an opinion such as Bellario's must be carefully prepared, after turning "o'er many books." It is a predetermined conclusion, based upon reported cases, as to the rights of the parties in a particular situation, as well as an indication of the proper course of procedure which, in this instance, Portia followed so successfully.

Shakespeare, through Bellario and Portia, disclosed the fact that he had access to many books similar to those used by the writer and, in searching through their pages or after consultation with those who had, he seemed to have reached the con-

---

[A] Sir William Dugdale, *Origines Juridiciales; or, Historical Memorials of English Laws, Courts of Justice,* p. 311.

[B] Holdsworth, *A History* . . . , Vol. VI, p. 450, note 5.

[C] See note 44.

clusion that the quibble of the pound of flesh, as found in *Il Pecorone* and perhaps in the play Gosson mentions, could be solved equitably and dramatically by "a young doctor from Rome," from whence also comes the term "equity" (*aequus*).

33. ". . . the Venetian law cannot impugn you as you do proceed."

Thus, we find Shakespeare, through this speech of Portia, reiterating the fact that Shylocke was entitled to the harsh penalty of his bond in the Court of King's Bench, for there was no defense available thereto at common law.

34. The "single bond" of Antonio.

This is what Blackstone says about Shylocke's "single bond" and its enforceability at the time the play was written and is not to be confused with what the same author has to say about the enforcement of such bonds at the present time:

1. An *obligation* or bond, is a deed whereby the obligor obliges himself . . . to pay a certain sum of money to another at a day appointed. If this be all, the bond is called a single one, *simplex obligatio;* but there is generally a condition added, that if the obligor does some particular act, the obligation shall be void, or else shall remain in full force: as . . . repayment of a principal sum of money borrowed of the obligee, with interest, which principal sum is usually one-half of the penal sum specified in the bond. In case this condition is not performed, the bond becomes forfeited, or absolute at law, and charges the obligor, while living. . . .[A]

[A] Blackstone, *Commentaries . . .* , Book II, p. 801.

As a matter of fact, Antonio did not execute the type of instrument that was first agreed upon, for the bond as finally drafted by Shylocke contained the forfeiture clause of a pound of flesh which made it a *duplex obligatio*. This act on the part of Shylocke could have been used as the basis of another equitable defense, namely, fraud and misrepresentation at the inception of a contract; but Shakespeare, through Portia, did not avail himself of it.

35. *Strictum jus*.

If we recall the traditional method of approach to the solution of a legal dispute, we shall better understand why equitable principles were unavailing in a law court. The judge, in a court of common law, had all of his faculties focused on five or six set forms of action or types of cases, such as debt, detinue, trover, replevin, trespass, etc. And he was constantly comparing or contrasting the case before him to the set type or traditional form under which it was being tried. If it did not conform in the most minute detail, he did not hesitate to act accordingly, regardless of the actual and apparent unfairness of his judgment. This is illustrated by a case that was tried before the Court of Common Pleas just ten years before *The Merchant of Venice* was written, the facts of which are as follows: A traveler came into a London inn—perhaps one of the very ones in which some of the early plays were enacted—and sought a night's lodging. The innkeeper failed to inform him of the sum that he would be charged for the occupancy of the room and the cost of his dinner and breakfast. The traveler failed to promise the innkeeper that he would pay for his accommodations. The traveler partook of all that the innkeeper offered in food and shelter and refused to pay his bill the next morning. The innkeeper sued at common law and all of the facts, just as I have stated them, were made known to the judge who decided the case in favor of the traveler. In so doing, the court informed the plaintiff that he had no suit in an action of debt because the sum involved was not fixed, certain, and agreed upon; that he had no suit in an action of assumpsit, for the defendant had not promised or agreed to pay the plaintiff a sum of money (Young vs. Asburnham, 3 Leo, p. 161. 1587).[A]

36. "The quality of mercy. . . ."

Portia's "quality of mercy" speech is perhaps the greatest equitable plea ever penned or spoken; but let us remember that the trial at law had not proceeded to judgment and that equitable principles were not considered by the common law judges in 1597 and were, therefore, of no avail in the Court of Common Pleas or the Court of King's Bench.

We must not be confused by the present meaning of justice and should realize that many in Shakespeare's audience knew that justice came from the Latin root *jus,* which meant a right or law and, therefore, in the "quality of mercy" speech was synonymous with the strict common law of England.

"Mercy"[B] is not a term so broad in its meaning and scope as *aequitas* (*L. aequus*) or equity but is the leaven which, when added to the tough dough of the common law, raises it to what Plato in his *Republic* described as an approach to an Ideal— which is law's approximation of the ultimate Good. When Immanuel Kant writes of the "universal reign of the moral law," he is not speaking of mercy but of the law of man softened by mercy and enlightened by Divine Intelligence. That is equity. It is the principle for which Thomas Carlyle was searching, and, realizing it could not be found in the Utilitarian Philosophy of Bentham or Mill, he ultimately discovered the essence of it in the idealistic literature of Germany. It is the antithesis of what Wordsworth abhors when he sees what man has made of man.

Aequitas is opposed to *strictum jus* and varies in meaning between reasonable modification of the letter and substantial justice. It is to be taken as a frame of mind in dealing with legal questions and not as a source of law.[C]

Let it not be thought for one instant from the description or definition of equity attempted above that it is an abstract, impotent force, for if one has the misfortune of obstructing its progress one finds, as Shylocke did, that it is an irresistible force that ultimately puts one into the proper place in the general scheme of things.

37. ". . . gentle rain from heaven. . . ."

No amount of eloquence or a plea of mercy, such as the young lawyer used in Antonio's defense, would have had any effect in the case cited in note 35. It had no place in such proceedings and therefore could not be given the slightest considera-

---

[A] See Holdsworth, *A History* . . . , Vol. III, pp. 446–447, for an English translation of the report.

[B] See also James Murray, *New English Dictionary.*

[C] John Bouvier, *Law Dictionary,* Vol. I, p. 157.

tion. The law was cut, quartered, dried, salted, and hung in the smokehouse of precedent where no "gentle rain from heaven" could "mitigate"[A] and spoil it.

To illustrate the influence that the increasing power and competition of the Court of Chancery were exerting on the common law, I cite the case of Warbrooke vs. Griffin (2 Brownlow 254, 1610).[B]

This case was decided twenty-three years after Asburnham's case on identical facts. In this instance, the court reached the conclusion that debt would not lie nor would assumpsit but that a combination of the two would constitute a cause of action for the plaintiff. The court in so holding broke a long tradition of at least four centuries and allowed a litigant to sue out two causes of action, or what amounted to two causes of action, simultaneously.

38. "Is he not able to discharge the money?"

The earliest intimation of the ultimate development of the bond or mortgage as a security transaction occurs in the following language of Justice Spigurnel in the case of Anon. vs. Anon. (1314):

When a man pledges tenements his intention is not to grant an estate of inheritance, but to give security for the repayment of the money he has borrowed and to redeem the tenements; and in such case, if he repay the money he can enter.[C]

Unfortunately, this ray of light upon the

security transaction and the equity of redemption thereto was immediately extinguished and did not appear again but for this fleeting instant in the work of Littleton:

. . . the money at the beginning trenched to the feoffee in manner as a dutie, and shall be intended that the estate was made by reason of the lending of the money by the feoffee, or for some other dutie; and therefore the payment shall not be made to his heir. . . .[D]

The next outcropping of this theory of a man's right to recover goods pledged, by repaying the sum borrowed, appears in the fourteenth year of the reign of Elizabeth in the case of Hide vs. Chowne.[E] This was the beginning of a precedent and not another isolated example as had been the utterances of Spigurnel in the fourteenth century and Littleton in the fifteenth century.

It is to this right to redeem goods pledged, so novel to the Elizabethans and yet so essential to the equitable solution of many cases, that Shakespeare refers when he has the young lawyer turn to Antonio's friend, Bassanio, and say, "Is he not able to discharge the money?" (208) (For a more detailed discussion of this point, see notes 70 and 71.)

39. "Yes, here I tender it for him in the court. . . ."

Tender is the correct technical term meaning a valid offer to deliver something,

---

[A] See also Murray, *op. cit.*
[B] See Holdsworth, *A History* . . . , Vol. III, p. 447.
[C] *Eyre of Kent* (Seld. Soc. Pub.), Vol. III, p. 85, quoted by W. F. Walsh, *A Treatise on Mortgages*, p. 6, note 16; Holdsworth, *A History* . . . , Vol. III, p. 130, note 5.

[D] Holdsworth, *A History* . . . , Vol. II, p. 579, note 10; Coke, . . . *a Commentary upon Littleton* . . . , Vol. II, Sect. 339.
[E] Monro, *Reports*, p. 395; see also Walsh, . . . *on Mortgages*, pp. 8–9, 11, notes 22–28, 30, for a collection of cases on this point.

made in pursuance of some contract, bond, or obligation, under such circumstances as to require no further act on the part of the one making the offer. Thus, we see Shakespeare using a very unusual term in its most appropriate place when he introduces the legal term "tender" rather than the nonlegal phrase "offer." It is the overtones and connotations of a word like "tender" that strike with singular force one schooled in those terms when the term itself is used correctly. Thus Coke, Bacon, and Ellesmere, who probably heard the play, must have been struck by the proper use of this and other legal terms and phrases to which I have called attention elsewhere.

40. "To do a great right, do a little wrong. . . ."

This is the stuff on which maxims are made: Shakespeare, the master of language, has caught in poetry, and thus made immortal, the long-recognized and oft-used prosaic term "balancing the equities." Is not Portia merely asked to put the merit of Shylocke's plea on one side of the balance and on the other to heap high its demerits, watch the beam, and prevail upon the court to see eye to eye with her?

41. "Decree" or "Judgment"?

Holdsworth thus states the difference between the nature and character of the decision rendered in the common law courts (judgments) and those rendered in equity courts (decrees) :

We have seen that in the common law courts the court simply decided the specific issue raised by the pleadings. In equity, on the other hand, the court considered the whole circumstances of the case made by the bill and answer, and tried to make a decree which would give effect to the rights of all the parties according to the circumstances of the case.[A]

In support of his contention he quotes Spence:

The judgments of the common law, following the writ on which the action was founded, were uniform simple and invariable, according to the nature of the action, as that the said William recover seisin, or his term of years, or his damages. . . . In the court of Chancery no writ or formula of action imposed any fetter of form; and the court, not being tied to forms, was able to modify the relief given by its decrees to answer all the particular exigencies of the case fully and circumstantially.[B]

Shakespeare here used an equitable term instead of the proper legal one, for there are decrees in equity and judgments at law. The former affect only the person of the defendant while the latter affect only his property; that is, decrees are *in personam* and judgments *in rem*. However, in lines 102 and 103 the terms are used by Shylocke in a manner clearly indicating that the dramatist knew and recognized their significance.

I call attention to this point because it is the one glaring exception to the dramatist's absolute adherence to the proper use of technical terms throughout the trial. This exception may be explained if we concede that Shakespeare, through Portia, was contemplating the merger of legal and equitable proceedings as we have them today and anticipated the diminishing im-

---

[A] Holdsworth, *A History* . . . , Vol. IX, p. 338.
[B] *Ibid.,* note 5.

portance of such distinctions. I here list a few of these terms, properly used, of which there are many: "proceed to judgment," "I tendered it," "cause in controversy," "decree," "use," "penalty," "forfeiture," "let me have judgment," "dismiss this court," "sealed," "single bond," "whether you'll admit him," "your grace," "he is furnished with my opinion," "proceed," "alter a decree," "recorded for a precedent," "error," "perjury," "bond," "forfeit," "intent and purpose of the law," "the court awards it," "a sentence," "prepare," "confiscate," "law," "act," "open court," "enacted," "alien," "citizen," "party," "pardon," "fine," "record a gift," "all he dies possessed," "pronounced," "draw a deed of gift," "deed," "when it is paid according to the tenour," "give judgment," "bankrupt," "oath," "mitigate," "justice of thy plea," "in the course of justice," "question in the court," "difference," "confess the bond," and "the law allows it."[A]

42. "The law allows it, and the court awards it."

At law, the judgment is yea or nay, for one party and against the other; . . . contains the conclusion of "the law upon the facts proved, and leaves the party to his legal and appropriate writ to enforce it."[B]

The judgment, though pronounced or awarded by the judges, is not their determination or sentence, but the determination and sentence of *the law*.

. . . .

All these species of judgments are either *interlocutory* or *final*. *Interlocutory* judgments are such as are given in the middle of a cause, upon some plea . . . which is only intermediate, and does not finally determine or complete the suit.[C]

Final judgments are such as at once put an end to the action. . . .[D]

It is true today, as it was in the time of Shakespeare, that no power can alter a judgment once it becomes final, but today, as in Elizabethan England, a Court of Chancery can by injunction prevent a party to a suit from exercising the legal rights of the judgment obtained therein. It is seeming paradoxes like this which have led many to speak of the trial scene of *The Merchant of Venice* as a resort to a legal quibble. This, however, is not a quibble nor is it a paradox. It is the result of the working of two great forces in our modern jurisprudence, and when they conflict or clash, unless we understand the fundamental principles of each, we are prone to misinterpret their differences.

43. ". . . the story of the living law. . . ."

The common law differs from all other systems of jurisprudence in that it has grown entirely from the slow accumulation of cases which were actually tried and decided, and, thus, the points of law contained therein have become precedents. The reports of these cases were collected in the *Eyres of Kent, Year Books,* and individual reports, such as those of Lord Chief Justice Coke, Cary, Tothill, Choyce, and others. They have been so often referred to, relied upon, quoted from, and used for the determination of similar cur-

---

[A] *The Merchant of Venice*, I, iii; IV, i.
[B] A. C. Freeman, *A Treatise of the Law of Judgments*, Vol. I, p. 3.

[C] Blackstone, *Commentaries* . . . , Book III, p. 1354.
[D] *Ibid.*, p. 1356.

rent cases that they have become the precedents for later cases and *are*, therefore, using the term literally, the common law.

The processes of centuries, by which these varied elements were amalgamated into an organic whole, are reflected in the collections of early statutes and in the yearbooks . . . and in the famous abridgments of Statham, Fitzherbert, and Brooke. . . . Thus we may follow on these printed pages, yellowed with age, the story of the living law, drawn from these diverse sources, as it gradually assumes a character of its own, develops into a whole greater than its parts, and becomes one of the two great systems of law which the world has known. Present-day problems seem remote from the life portrayed by these ancient texts, yet if one has the patience to follow the tortuous path of their law French . . . , he will be reminded that the substance of life has changed less through the centuries than we are accustomed to think.[A]

It is the fear of establishing an erroneous precedent which would be followed *ad infinitum* of which Portia is mindful when she says that it would be impossible for anyone to alter a judgment at law after it has been formally entered into the public records of the state and thereby has become a final judgment.

44. " 'Twill be recorded for a precedent. . . ."

The duty of a judge with reference to reported cases is

. . . to abide by former precedents, *stare decisis,* where the same points come again in litigation, as well as to keep the scale of justice even and steady, and not liable to waver with every new judge's opinion, as also because, the law in that case being solemnly declared and determined, what was before uncertain, and perhaps indifferent, is now

become a permanent rule, which it is not in the breast of any subsequent judge to alter or swerve from according to his private sentiments; he being sworn to determine, not according to his own private judgment, but according to the known laws and customs of the land,—not delegated to pronounce a new law, but to maintain and expound the old one—*jus dicere et non jus dare.*[B]

From this very accurate and illuminating definition of *stare decisis*, one can easily see why Selden, who believed absolutely, totally, and completely in the doctrine, *jus dicere et non jus dare,* called equity "a roguish thing" because it had no measure more constant than the Chancellor's foot.[C]

45. ". . . this strict court of Venice. . . ."

The common law, if examined in the perspective of ten centuries, shows certain clearly defined growth rings as does the cross section of a giant redwood; and one who is skilled in reading these lines can tell the periods of drought and plenty in the common law, just as plainly as such periods are determinable by the relative magnitude of the cross section of the growth rings of a tree. Thus, when we find less than a normal amount of litigation, we know that the common law is in one of its inflexible stages; that soon a change will come; and that there will be ever so slight a relaxation from the strict common law forms of action, at which time perhaps some clever lawyer will also devise some ruse by which this rigidity can be avoided; or perhaps the sheer weight of social, eco-

---

[A] Harlan Fiske Stone, introduction to *Legal Manuscripts and Printed Books,* Huntington Library.

[B] Herbert Broom, *Legal Maxims,* pp. 147–148.
[C] See note 13.

nomic, or political forces, as in the reign of Elizabeth, will cause a period of extraordinary development and growth. During such a period there is a great burst of litigation, and the common law, as the crab when his shell is soft, grows rapidly to adapt itself to new conditions. The fourteenth and fifteenth centuries were hard-shelled so far as law was concerned, but a new period of growth and development was dawning. The following quotation illustrates the inflexibility of the common law in the fifteenth century:

> Thus in the fifteenth century the maker of a bond for double the amount of his debt would be compelled at law, if he had left the bond uncanceled in the hands of his creditor, to pay the full amount of the bond, though he had paid his debt, as the law admitted no parol evidence of payment as a defense to the bond. In such cases equity compelled the surrender and cancellation of the bond.[A]

46. "Why, this bond is forfeit. . . ."

Two conditions precedent to a suit on such bonds were that the debt was past due and the sum specified in the bond unpaid. Thus was a bond forfeit and, being forfeit, became the basis of a cause of action at law.

Shakespeare shows his familiarity with this point, for it takes but a glance at the instrument itself on the part of Portia to convince her that the bond actually is forfeit and therefore an instrument which is enforceable at common law.

FORFEITURE OF A BOND. A failure to perform the condition upon which the obligee was to be excused from the penalty in the bond.[B] The word forfeiture includes not merely the idea of losing the penalty, but also of having the property right transferred to the other party, without the consent of the party who has violated his obligation. Where the enforcement of a forfeiture was unjust, courts of equity always granted relief therefrom,[C] and courts of law finally came to assume a like jurisdiction.[D,E]

47. "The penalty and forfeit of my bond."

The customary penalty at this time in such bonds was twice the sum borrowed.

Doubtless, many of those gaily bedecked gentlemen of Shakespeare's audience, who sat in the most expensive seats upon the very stage, knew from personal experience the fear and dread of having to raise five hundred pounds by a certain day or be incarcerated in the Fleet until, what was more than twice as difficult, a thousand pounds could be raised to satisfy the usurer.[F]

It was remarked by Lord Bacon, in one of his Essays, that people were wont to say that it was " 'gainst nature, for money to beget money"; Antonio expresses this same thought in his philosophy that friendship would not exact a breed for barren metal. He asked no special favor or courtesy, but only that in case he failed to keep his bond, that the penalty be exacted.

A penalty is the undertaking to pay an additional sum of money or to submit to punishment of a certain kind, if there shall be a failure to fulfill the

---

[B] Bouvier, *op. cit.*, Vol. II, p. 1282.

[C] Coke, . . . *a Commentary upon Littleton* . . . Vol. II, Sect. 339; 2 Bl. Comm., p. 340.

[D] *Ibid.*

[E] White, *op. cit.*, p. 121.

[F] The writer is indebted to G. W. Keeton, *Shakespeare and His Legal Problems*, p. 16, for the allusion to contemporary playgoers.

[A] Barbour, *History of Contracts in Early English Equity*, Oxford Studies, Vol. IV, p. 89, quoted by Walsh, . . . *on Mortgages*, p. 7.

contract obligation. The term is mostly applied to pecuniary punishment, but may as well include the corporal punishment included in the obligation of this bond, in case of a breach of its condition.[A]

48. ". . . bid me tear the bond."

Shylocke's suit at law rested entirely upon his ability to produce the sealed bond in court, and if it were destroyed or cancelled he would have no basis for his suit. Doubtless, Shakespeare is playing upon this fact and another equally as well-known to the Elizabethans, namely, that the three methods of cancelling an instrument of this kind which were recognized by the common law courts were by writing cancelled across the face of the instrument, by tearing, or by burning the instrument. Since the right to sue on such bonds was based on the form of the instrument and not the intent of the parties as expressed therein, the common law judges reasoned that the right to sue on such instruments was lost even though the bond were torn or burned, not with the intent to cancel but by accident.[B]

49. "When it is paid according to the tenour."

This is another example of the correct use of a legal term which means so much to one accustomed to use words for nice distinctions.

When Shylocke uttered this legal phrase, it must have sent shudders through Eliza-

bethan audiences for they knew that to pay the bond "according to the tenour" (235) meant payment according to the purport and effect of the instrument, and death to Antonio.

50. "For the intent and purpose of the law Hath full relation to the penalty."

Bouvier defines liquidated damages as follows:

Where there is an agreement between parties for the doing or not doing particular acts, the parties may, if they please, estimate beforehand the damages to result from a breach of the agreement, and prescribe in the agreement itself the sum to be paid by either by way of damages for such breach.[C]

51. "A sentence! Come, prepare!"

Lord Chief Justice Coke must have considered the usual form of judgment on a bond commonplace and unworthy of mention in his great treatise on the common law, for in the section of his . . . *a Commentary upon Littleton* . . . entitled "of Judgments and Executions," this form is not included. I have, however, selected the following judgment which will suffice to illustrate my point:

Judgement in Case of Misprision of High Treason.

That the offender by the common law shall for this concealment forfeit all his goods; and the profits of his lands during his life, and suffer imprisonment during his life.[D]

[A] White, *op. cit.*, p. 112.
[B] See also the quotation from Walsh, . . . *on Mortgages*, p. 7, in note 45.

[C] Bouvier, *op. cit.*, Vol. II, p. 2024.
[D] Coke, . . . *a Commentary upon Littleton* . . . , Third Part, Ch. 101, p. 217.

52. "Execution adjudged."

Gardiner vs. Bullard *alias* Bullward, Hilary. Queen's Bench K.B. 27/1296/289 D. 1586.

Gardiner says that he recently recovered, by judgment, £17:1s. against John Bullard *alias* Bullward, but that execution remains to be done. And since Martin Manley of Bermondsey, leatherseller, and John Luce, of Newington, gentleman, in Easter term, 26 Eliz. (1584), came into this Court and became pledges for Bullard, and Bullard neither paid nor went to prison, Gardiner seeks execution against the pledges. Execution adjudged.[A]

53. ". . . il ne poit avoir remedy per nostre Ley."

It had become possible, more than one hundred years before the case at bar, for one of the litigants to appeal to the Chancellor for relief from a judgment at common law. The customary manner of appeal was for the unsuccessful litigant to go into the Court of Chancery and there state to the Chancellor the reasons why he had not received a fair decision at law. This statement of such reasons was called an exception, and when later it was written it became known as a "bill of exception" (M.P. vs. J.R., *Year Books*, 37 Henry VI, [1459], plea 3).[B]

The full title to the *Year Book* just cited above is *La premiere part des ANS du ROY HENRY le VI a nouvellement perusee, & Corigee, avec les marginal notes.* This book is written, as are the other *Year*

Books, in a mixture of Norman French, Latin, and English.

54. ". . . moults choses sont etre suis icy que ne sont remediables a le common ley. . . ."

M.P. vs. J.R., *Year Books*, 37 Henry VI, plea 4. The facts of this case are as follows: One named M.P., who lived in London, agreed to buy from one J.R. certain debts due him (J.R.), and for these debts M.P. promised under seal to pay the price agreed upon. The debts were *choses in action* and by law at that time were not transferable, so M.P. had got no *quid pro quo* for his promise to pay. As, however, the promise was executed under seal, M.P. was liable on it and bound thereby at common law. M.P. in order to protect himself appealed to the Chancellor. This was a novel problem for the Chancellor, in 1459, and one of great importance. He, therefore, adjourned the case[c] until it could be heard in the Exchequer Chamber where sat all of the judges of both common law courts and the Chancery Court. After much discussion and deliberation it was agreed that since M.P. had got nothing for his promise he ought in equity to be released, and J.R. was ordered to cancel the bond. J.R., after this proceeding and decree, not only did not cancel the bond but brought suit on it at common law. The Chancellor then issued an injunction and ordered M.P. to the Fleet, the prison for debtors, for contempt of his decree.

The opinion of Prisot of the common law court seems to have been that, while the proceedings in chancery were in good

---

[A] Hotson, *op. cit.*, p. 217.

[B] The writer suggests the reading of this case in translation, for it has many factual points in common with Shylocke vs. Antonio, and the legal and equitable principles involved are, in most respects, identical.

[c] See note 20.

conscience, J.R. might, at the risk of being incarcerated, disregard the injunction if he so desired.[A]

In *Year Books*, 4 Henry VII, there is a case reported, tried in 1489, which shows the development of the power of equity in thirty years. In that case Judge Finneux held that.

> Every law should be in accordance with the law of God, and I know well that an executor who fraudulently misapplies the goods and does not make restitution will be damned in Hell and to remedy this is, as I understand it, in accordance with conscience.[B]

Three years later the judges of the common law agreed in a case similar to M.P. vs. J.R. that the one who had promised to give something for nothing would not be forced to fulfill his promise even though it were under seal and that he could be relieved therefrom in equity because there was no remedy at common law.[C]

Thus, we see in three cases, one of which in many respects is similar to Antonio's

case, the use of a device which the young lawyer in Antonio's case has taken advantage of, namely, an appeal to the Court of Chancery for relief from a judgment at law.

55. "It was then usual to grant injunctions on surmises. . . ."

The following case illustrates the fact that equity had so developed by 1597 that the Chancellor could and did grant an injunction to become effective *when and if* a certain designated event occurred:

> CHRISTOPHERUS *v.* CHOMELY
> *Injunction with a clause (si ita sit).*—An injunction was granted to the plaintant, upon the surmises of his bill, with the clause (*si ita sit*). . . . *Nota,* it was then usual to grant instructions upon surmises, with a proviso (*si ita sit*). . . . (Anno 1 Eliz. fol. 67 [1558–59]).[D]

56. ". . . writ of error. . . ."

The first step in the appeal of a case at common law is thus described by Blackstone:

> . . . the principal method of redress for erroneous judgments in the king's court of record is by *writ of error* to some superior court of appeal. . . . The writ of error only lies upon matters of *law* arising upon the face of the proceedings; so that no evidence is required to substantiate or support it. . . .[E]

57. "Injunction to stay suits at Common Law."

In the cases taken from *Year Books*, 7 Henry VII, Paschae Term, plea 8, the

---

[A] The pertinent part of Judge Prisot's opinion is as follows: "*Quand le fait est bon et tout temps ad este, lour examinacion ne fera ceo mauveis, mes lour examinacion ne prove le fait bon et loyal en nostre Ley: et pur tant que il ne poit avoir remedy per nostre Ley, il suira la pur estre restore al obligacion; et cest l'effect de lour pouvoir et lour judgement, a restorer la party al obligation, ou a faire la party a faire acquit, ou a executer, ceo ne poit la court la rien faire, sinon commander luy al prison, etre la tanque il veut ce faire: et issint cest tout que le dit Court poit faire.*" *Year Books*, 37 Henry VI, Hillarii Term, p. 14, plea 3; Holdsworth, *A History* . . . , Vol. V, p. 221, note 1.

[B] Holdsworth, *A History* . . . , Vol. V, p. 222, note 2. "*La Ley de la terre est pur moults choses, et moults choses sont etre sues icy que ne sont remediables a le Common Ley, et assez sont en conscience parentre un homme et son confesseur, et issint est cest chose.*" *Year Books*, 4 Henry VII, Hillarii Term, p. 4, plea 8.

[C] Holdsworth, *A History* . . . , Vol. V, p. 222, note 5. "*Et issint si on paye un duty d'un obligation ed n'ad escrit, ceo est bon conscience; et uncore al Common Ley nul barre.*" *Year Books*, 7 Henry VII, Paschae Term, p. 12, plea 2.

[D] *The English Reports*, Vol, 21, p. 20.
[E] Blackstone, *Commentaries* . . . , Book III, p. 363.

Chancellor issued an injunction restraining the defendant (who was the plaintiff in the suit at law), at his own risk, from exercising the right of enforcing his contract at common law; but in the earlier case the common law judge said that his court would not be influenced by the equitable decree and, therefore, he would not support it by his judgment. Thus, the plaintiff could assert his common law rights at his own peril. In the later case, the judge decided to follow the dictates of equity and render judgment for the defendant on the contract at common law, thus completely defeating the cause of the plaintiff.

The following cases selected from *The English Reports* are examples of injunctive relief against a judgment, or an impending judgment, at common law:

THOROUGHGOOD *v.* MAY.

Injunction to stay suits at Common Law.—The defendant, since the bill exhibited, commenced several suits at the common law for the cause here complained of against the plaintant, and his under-tenants; therefore an injunction is awarded against him. . . .[A] [1578–79]

COTES *v.* FRESTON.

An Injunction to stay Execution.—A Writ is awarded against the Defendant, his Counsellors, and Attorneys, that they upon the penalty of £100 shall sue no execution of a Judgement in an Action of debt commenced by the Defendant against the Plaintiff at common Law, until further order be taken therein by this Court of Chancery.[B]

AYLAND *v.* FRANCIS BACON.

Injunction to stay proceedings in judgment or execution.—An injunction is awarded against the defendant, to stay his proceedings in the Sheriff's Court, of London, or elsewhere, upon debt of one

hundred pounds, not to proceed to trial, judgment, or to execution, if judgment be given. . . .[C] [1558]

These cases illustrate the striking fact that one party to a suit at common law could, after judgment had been rendered or before the final judgment, resort to equity for injunctive relief against such judgment. One case cited illustrates the more striking point of the use of an injunction to prevent even the bringing of a suit at law.

It, therefore, seems quite natural to me, as it did to Shakespeare's Elizabethan audiences, to have the final pronouncement of a judgment at law followed by Portia's next remark, "Tarry a little; there is something else." (305) This "something else" was a resort to the relief which equity afforded to litigants who found themselves in a situation similar to that of Antonio.

58. "Sure there cannot be a greater solecism. . . ."

The predicament in which Shylocke found himself was novel but not unique; that is, it was a comparatively new development of jurisprudence. But Shylocke was not the only one who felt the restraining leash of the injunction, even after he had a valid judgment at law. As a matter of fact, that most commonplace phrase of today, "It is being done," applies more accurately to this situation than any other phrase that one can call to mind. The usual procedure in 1597 was for the unsuccessful defendant to rush from the court of law to the Chancellor and there plead for the protection of equity against the relentless application of the principles of the common law through which the judges ground out

---

[A] *The English Reports,* Vol. 21, p. 60.
[B] *Ibid.,* p. 67.
[C] *Ibid.,* p. 19.

justice according to its letter and not its spirit. After much research, I found the three following reports of one case which illustrate this procedure, from beginning to end, step by step.

[1] STANEBRIDGE *v.* HALES.

Injunction to stay all proceedings at common law. An injunction was granted against the defendant upon pain of one hundred pounds, that he should not prosecute an action of debt of five [*sic*] pounds, or any writ of *nisi prius*, jury, judgment, or execution of judgment, if judgment be given, before the Justices of either Bench, until special licence be given by this Court: Thomas Stanebridge, plaintant; Thomas Hales, defendant (Anno 1 Eliz. fol. 103. [1558–59]) .[A]

[2] STANEBRIDGE *v.* HALES.

Injunction to stay suits if the plaintant bring £223 into Court; execution to stay for the rest.— It is ordered, the injunction formerly granted (48) against the defendant, for stay of his action in the King's Bench be dissolved, and the defendant to be at liberty to take judgment upon his action of debt of five hundred pounds. Provided if the plaintant do bring into Court on Monday next, two hundred and twenty-three pounds, then execution for the rest is to be suspended until this court take order: Thomas Stanebridge, plaintant; Thomas Hales, defendant (Anno 2 Eliz. fol. 176. [1559–60]) .[B]

[3] HALES *v.* STANEBRIDGE.

Injunction dissolved if cause be not shewed.— It is ordered, if the defendant shew not cause on Friday next, then the injunction before granted for the defendant against the plaintant, to stay his execution in the King's Bench, shall be dissolved, or else the money for which the plaintant lieth in execution at the defendant's suit shall remain in his hands, in part of payment of such money as is due unto him by the defendant; and afterwards upon Friday, because the Lord Keeper did not sit in Court to hear such cause as was offered, further day was given, and afterwards the plaintant was left at liberty to call (50) for execution upon the judgment, because the defendant

shewed no cause: Thomas Hales, plaintant; Thomas Stanebridge, defendant (Anno 2 Eliz. fol. 244. [1559–60]) .[C]

On the practice of granting injunctions against the enforcement of judgments of courts of common law prevalent at the close of the sixteenth century, Blackstone says:

And sure there cannot be a greater solecism, than that in two sovereign independent courts established in the same country, exercising concurrent jurisdiction, and over the same subject-matter, there should exist in a single instance two different rules of property, clashing with or contradicting each other.[D]

Is it not reasonable to conclude from the three cases cited and the quotation from Blackstone that Shakespeare, who was probably one of the most sensitive of all the Elizabethans to topics of current interest, was foreshadowing a similar situation when Shylocke says:

There is no force in the decrees of Venice.
I stand for judgment: answer; shall I have it? [102]

59. ". . . thou shalt see the difference of our spirits. . . ."

Here the entire spirit of the trial changes, and the shift is an abrupt one from the use of legal principles to those of equity. From this point on, the scene is unmistakably laid in a Court of Chancery. In refraining from actually changing the scene, and thus depicting a suit at law and hearing in chancery as one continuous proceeding, Shakespeare very cleverly heightened the dramatic effect.[E] Law and equity courts

---

[A] *Ibid.,* p. 24.
[B] *Ibid.,* p. 26.

[C] *Ibid.,* p. 27.
[D] Blackstone, *Commentaries* . . . , Book III, p. 1395.
[E] The writer acknowledges his indebtedness to Keeton, *op. cit.,* p. 18, for the statement as to the dramatic effect of the scene.

were combined in England, two hundred and seventy-six years after this trial scene was enacted, by the Judicature Act of 1873, and Shakespeare's combination of the proceedings, an innovation unwarranted by the practice of his own time, is a poetic and prophetic anticipation of what was to become the common and usual procedure.

To support my contention that the entire scene of this trial shifts from a court of law to a Court of Chancery, I advance the following points:

1. The trial at law ends, as all trials do, with the pronouncement and entry of the final judgment which in this instance is as follows:

A pound of that same merchant's flesh is thine:
The court awards it, and the law doth give it.

. . . .

And you must cut this flesh from off his breast:
The law allows it, and the court awards it. [299]

2. The next speech of Portia, "Tarry a little; there is something else," (305) indicates that the litigation is not concluded but there is more to follow. Then is presented the equitable theory of the prevention of waste by the use of an injunction, for Portia, speaking for the court, reiterates that Shylocke is entitled to his pound of flesh but that in the taking thereof his action is at his own peril.

3. Portia then illustrates a procedure in equity, very different from that of common law, by which the Chancellor decides not only the one issue put before him by the pleadings but also all the various aspects of the case in such a way that a fair and reasonable solution of the entire controversy is made. This exemplifies the power of equity, after once having assumed jurisdiction, to exercise that jurisdiction for complete disposition of the controversy as

illustrated by the Chancellor's application of the penal statute.

4. When Bassanio and the court are told that Shylocke can no longer claim the sum offered in redemption of the bond because he has previously denied his right thereto, Portia propounds the equitable principles of Estoppel. (338)

5. Shakespeare then makes use of the complete jurisdiction of chancery by having Portia produce a statute, according to the terms of which Antonio as informer for the state is entitled to one-half of the goods of Shylocke. The Chancellor, as the Duke should now be called, does not hesitate to decide this aspect of the case by the dictates of equity and good conscience. (348 *et seq.*)

6. The Chancellor's first words after the judgment at law are "Thou shalt see the difference of our spirits." (368) This remark is made to Shylocke who, throughout the trial, has repeatedly said, "I stand here for law." (142) It is my contention that Portia and the Duke, after he represents the Chancellor, stand for equity.

7. We next have an illustration of the flexibility of a decree in chancery as contrasted to the rigidity of a judgment at law, for the Chancellor first indicates the probable form which his decree will take and adds that he will alter it to a simple fine if Shylocke is sufficiently humble. (372) He then listens to the plea of the opposing litigant and decides to make a further change in his decree before its final entry. (391 *et seq.*)

8. Shakespeare concludes the scene with the final decree of the Chancellor in which he resorts to the creation of an equitable estate which was not recognized at common law, viz., the creation of a trust where-

in the legal title of property is placed in one person and the equitable title to the same property rests in another. (388 *et seq.*) The disposition of Antonio's one-half of Shylocke's estate also illustrates the equitable conveyance of *a use after a use.* (382 *et seq.*)

9. The Chancellor does not act *in rem* on the property of the defendant but, as equity always acts, *in personam.* This is shown most vividly by his last official statement which he addresses to Shylocke: "Get thee gone, but do it." (397)

Thus, Shakespeare forsakes the rigid, inflexible procedure at law and turns to the more plastic and effective equitable devices for the ultimate solution of the bond plot. The points referred to above will be treated in detail as they occur at the hearing in the Court of Chancery.

60. Injunction granted to stay irreparable injury.

BUSH *v.* FIELD.

The defendant stayed, by injunction, to pull down rooms, to *the prejudice of another's rooms.*—The plaintant sheweth, by his bill, that his house and the defendant's are joining together, and supported by one main wall, standing partly upon the freehold of either of the said parties; and the plaintant having also an entry, garret, and other necessary rooms standing upon the kitchen of the defendant, he the defendant went about to pull down the said wall, and thereby to overthrow the said garret; the defendant made title to some of the upper rooms, and hath pulled down part of the wall; an injunction is awarded to stay the defendant, to pull down any more of the wall, or any other part of the said house, whereby the said upper rooms may be overthrown, or impaired, until the matter be heard: Bush, plaintant; Field, defendant (Anno 22 Eliz. [1579–80]) .[A]

[A] *The English Reports,* Vol. 21, p. 48.

61. *"Injunction to stay all proceedings at common law."*

The Chancellor always allowed a temporary injunction,[B] if the plaintant's cause was worthy and the impending injury irreparable, even though the defendant to the suit in chancery was not present. These temporary injunctions, whether they were issued to restrain a successful litigant at common law or to restrain one who did not resort to law, were all effective for a limited time only; if the one seeking the injunctive relief showed good cause, at a formal hearing such injunction could be *made perpetual.*[C]

Thus, we see that the Chancellor could act effectively, for a limited time at least, without even the presence of both parties to a suit; and his decree could be made effective permanently by the one seeking relief without the presence of the other party, if the absent party was given notice of the issuance of the injunction. This notice could be actual; that is, the absent party could be informed directly by an officer of the court, or such notice could be left at his last known lodgings as shown by the following case:

BODMAN *v.* MORGAN.

Injunction left at the defendant's house and disobeyed, an attachment[D] *is awarded.*—Thomas Jones made oath, that a writ of injunction was left at the house of the defendant; and the plaintant maketh oath, the defendant hath proceeded in a suit in the King's Bench contrary to an injunc-

---

[B] See note 58, case 1.

[C] *The English Reports,* Vol. 21, p. 27, Hales vs. Stanebridge. For authority for the above statement, see note 58 which contains the case entitled, "Injunction dissolved if cause be not shewed."

[D] A court order to apprehend and imprison the party named herein for contempt.

tion; therefore an attachment: Bodman, plaintant; Morgan, defendant (Anno 22 Eliz. [1579–80]).[A]

62. *"Injunction dissolved if cause be not shewed."*

No litigant who sought the protection of the Court of Chancery by means of an injunction could make such relief permanent without a formal hearing. At this hearing it was customary for the Chancellor to dissolve the temporary injunction and thereby allow the other party to proceed, unless the plaintant produced sufficient evidence to convince the Chancellor that the temporary injunction should be made permanent.[B]

63. The analogy between bonds and mortgages.

There seems to have been no real difference in point of time or otherwise between relief from forfeiture in bond cases and in mortgage cases other than what was purely fortuitous.[C]

Thus the relief afforded to mortgagors who had failed to perform the condition and suffered forfeiture to take place in consequence followed upon the same lines as the relief given in the case of bonds.[D]

64. An act of waste.

At the end of the fourteenth century, it was quite clear in the minds of those learned in the law that a mortgagee in possession had an estate in land somewhat similar to that of a tenant for years which is, generally speaking, the interest of the lessee today. This estate for years was less than a life estate, and the judges, therefore, reasoned that one having the lesser estate should be governed by the same rules as the possessor of a life estate and, therefore, was entitled to take reasonable "botes" and "estovers" without committing waste. The tenant for years could, however, cut only underbrush for firewood and larger timber to keep the property in repair without committing waste. He was held accountable for all the timber on the estate and could not cut it for any other purpose.[E]

65. "Why doth the Jew pause? take thy forfeiture."

. . . equity did not prevent the mortgagee from taking or recovering possession, . . . but that it gave effect to the mortgagor's substantial rights as owner by charging the mortgagee as constructive trustee, compelling him to account for all rents and profits received by him from the property, and charging him with the duty to conserve and protect the property.[F]

The Court decreed money to the plaintiff against the defendant, albeit he had judgment and execution, being upon the point of usurious contract, and a lease being become forfeited, and the mortgagee devised the same to infants. The Court was of opinion that the plaintiff should have it again, paying the money. Langford and Barnard, 37 Eliz. and 28. [1594–96].[G]

[A] *The English Reports*, Vol. 21, p. 54.

[B] See note 58, case 3, for the authority for this statement.

[C] Walsh, . . . *on Mortgages*, p. 8; see also pp. 8–11, notes 22–30.

[D] R. W. Turner, *The Equity of Redemption*, p. 26; see also pp. 24–28 and notes.

[E] *Year Books*, 21 Henry VI, Paschae Term, p. 47, plea 23; 20 Edward III, pp. 402–412, plea 1. See also *The English Reports*, Vol. 78 (King's Bench Division, Book VII), p. 267, Foster vs. Leonard.

[F] Walsh, . . . *on Mortages*, pp. 100–101; see also note 25 and references contained therein.

[G] *The English Reports*, Vol. 21, p. 146.

The first quotation is from Walsh's recent book on mortgages, and the second is taken directly from the case cited therein.

From these quotations the following deductions are obvious:

1. Equity did not prevent the mortgagee from exercising his common law right to possession of the property pledged.
2. This right of possession could be exercised before or after forfeiture.
3. The mortgagee or pledgee in possession was held to a strict accounting of all of the rents and profits received from the estate.
4. He was charged with the duty to conserve and protect the property for the owner.
5. Even if the property became forfeited and was sold to another, the mortgagee in possession was accountable to the mortgagor for it and, upon payment of the money borrowed, was ordered to reacquire it and surrender it to the mortgagor.

Thus, it did not seem unreasonable or incongruous to Shakespeare's audience when they heard Portia repeatedly insist that Shylocke was entitled to his pound of flesh but that he would be held to strict account for any injury to Antonio in the taking thereof.

66. "Thyself shalt see the act. . . ."

The Statute of Gloucester

It is provided that a man from henceforth shall have a Writ of Waste in the Chancery against him that holdeth by the law of England or otherwise for term of life or for term of years. . . . And he which shall be attainted of waste shall lose the thing that he hath wasted, and moreover shall recompense thrice so much as the waste shall be taxed at. [6 Edward I, c. 5, 1278.][A]

In discussing this doctrine of waste, and the statute quoted above, Holdsworth says:

The Year Books contain many decisions upon the effect of the enactments. These decisions are the basis of the modern law upon this subject.[B]

One of the earliest cases wherein an injunction was granted to prevent waste occurs in Moore, from which Lord Ellesmere, at the close of the sixteenth century, quotes the following passage with approval:

Tenant pur vie, le remainder pur vie, le remainder ouster en fee, per que le waste en le primer tenant pur vie est dispunishable per le common ley: uncore ad estre decree in Chancery per l'advice des Judges sur complaint de cestuy en remainder en fee, que le primer tenant ne faire waste, et injunction la grant.[C]

Waste done by one which held by covenant [bond under seal], therefore, not punishable by law, yet holpen here. Songhurst *contra* Dixy, Tothill 188.[D]

If the Lord Chancellor in Shylocke vs. Antonio had not been of a nature more disposed to pardon than allow the commission of a wrong, he could have permitted Shylocke to exact the penalty of his bond and then in turn could have demanded of Shylocke three-fold the amount of his excess.

67. Equity acts only *in personam.*

The method by which the Chancery succeeded in effecting these various modifications of the rigidity of the law was by addressing orders to the parties concerned and by committing them and sometimes their legal advisers, to prison, for contempt in case of disobedience. [Holdsworth, *History of English Law,* Vol. V, p. 335.][E]

This power is graphically illustrated by

[A] Holdsworth, *A History* . . . , Vol. III, p. 121, note 8.

[B] *Ibid.,* p. 122.
[C] *King's Bench Reports,* p. 554, plea 748.
[D] *The English Reports,* Vol. 21, p. 164.
[E] The writer has quoted *in toto* Holdsworth, *A History* . . . , Vol. V, pp. 335–338, in Appendix I for the benefit of those who cannot avail themselves of this fine work.

the case of Allan vs. Dingley (19 Elizabeth [1576–77]).[A]

For a most illuminating exposition of the dexterity of the Chancellor and the many devices used to force obedience to his decree see Mr. Bickersteth's testimony before the Chancery Commission of 1826.[B]

68. ". . . power to commit for contempt. . . ."

The Chancellor by means of the writ of subpoena and his power to commit for contempt exercised strict control over the persons of all parties to a suit. He could order them to act in any way he saw fit. . . . It was because he was able to exercise this control that he was able to give remedies which the common law courts could not give.[C]

Therefore, it was not unusual for the Chancellor to resort to any device of law or equity that served his purpose. He could, as he did in Shylocke's case, force one litigant to forego his rights at law, simultaneously spare the same litigant from the harsh punishment specified in a statute, decree that a trust be created and a gift be recorded with the final admonition: "Get thee gone, but do it." (397)

69. "Thou shalt have justice, more than thou desirest."

The Court of equity having acquired cognizance of the suit for the purpose of discovery, will entertain it for the purpose of relief.[D]

After a court of equity has once got possession of a cause, it will not suffer any of the litigating parties to resort to another tribunal.[E]

The principles quoted above are almost as old as equity itself and were recognized in the sixteenth century; therefore, it was not unusual for the Court of Chancery in Shakespeare's time to adjudicate a penal statute if the court had once entertained jurisdiction of the "cause in controversy." (156)

70. "Is he not able to discharge the money?"

The first cases where the Chancellor gave relief to a mortgagor who had failed to pay on a stated day, (a relief which developed later into the mortgagor's equity of redemption), occurred in the reign of Elizabeth.[F]

This new species of relief seems to have arisen out of the relief which the Chancellors began to give against forfeitures of bonds of all kinds.[G]

The following cases are reported by Monroe in support of this development: Hide vs. Chowne (1572), Franclyn vs. Watkins (1579), Brown vs. Whentworth (1593).

A "bond" is an obligation in writing and under seal. Formerly, on the forfeiture of a bond, the whole penalty was recoverable at law, but in courts of equity—where forfeitures were relieved against —on breach of an obligation for payment of money only, the court would compel an acceptance of the original sum, with interest and deny the penalty, and, finally, on this practice becoming general in courts of law, as well, a statute was enacted, in England, providing that a tender of principal and interest with accrued costs, would operate as a full satisfaction of a bond.[H]

[A] *The English Reports*, Vol. 21, p. 70.

[B] *Parlt. Papers*, Vol. XV, App. A, p. 150 (1826).

[C] Holdsworth, *A History . . .* , Vol. I, p. 458; see also 458 *et seq*. for discussion on conflict of law and equity.

[D] John W. M. Fonblanque, *Equity*, Book I, Ch. I, Sect. 3.

[E] G. T. Bispham, *Principles of Equity*, Part III, Ch. II, Sect. 414.

[F] Turner, *op. cit.*, p. 24.

[G] *Ibid.*

[H] White, *op. cit.*, p. 123.

71. The Equity of Redemption.

If a man be bound in a penalty to pay money at a day and place,[A] by obligation, and intending to pay the same, is robbed by the way; or hath intreated by word some other respite at the hands of the obligee, or cometh short of the place by any misfortune; and so failing of payment, doth nevertheless provide and tender the money in short time after; in these, and many such like cases, the Chancery will compel the obligee to take his principal, with some reasonable consideration of his damages.

. . . the like favour is extendable against them that will take advantage upon any strict condition, for undoing the estate of another in lands, upon a small or trifling default. [1610][B]

Thus was the law summarized thirteen years after *The Merchant of Venice* was written. Had Portia desired it, Shylocke probably would have been allowed to accept the sum tendered him by Bassanio. But Shakespeare, perhaps for dramatic reasons, chose otherwise and thereby made use of an equitable estoppel for he has Portia say:

He hath refused it in open court:
He shall have merely justice and his bond. [338]

72. "He hath refused it in the open court: . . ."

WAIVER. "The relinquishment or refusal to accept of a right."[C]

[A] "If you repay me not on such a day,
    In such a place, such sum or sums as are
    Express'd in the condition. . . ." [147 *et seq.*]
[B] Holdsworth, *A History* . . . , Vol. V, p. 330; Turner, *op. cit.*, p. 25.
[C] Bouvier, *op. cit.*, Vol. III, p. 3417.

73. "He shall have nothing but the penalty."

In the sixteenth century, a statement made by either party to a sealed instrument was deemed conclusive proof of the facts contained therein. Therefore, either party relying upon the instrument was bound by it and estopped from denying the validity and effect of its terms and conditions.

"Estoppe," commeth of the French word *estoupe,* from whence the English word stopped: and it is called an estoppel or conclusion, because a man's owne act or acceptance stoppeth or closeth up his mouth. . . : and *Littleton's* case here proveth this description.

Touching estoppels, which is an excellent and curious kinde of learning, it is to be observed, that there be three kinde of estoppels, viz. by matter of record, by matter in writing, and by matter *in paiis.* [1595][D]

The following is one of the earliest illustrations of this point:

Anything contained in writing cannot by any exception of the parties be removed. [1293][E]

74. "Thou shalt have nothing but the forfeiture,
To be so taken at thy peril. . . ."

Once more the point is made that Shylocke was not forbidden to enforce his judgment at common law and take the penalty of his bond but was enjoined from injuring the defendant in so doing.

[D] Coke, . . . *a Commentary upon Littleton* . . . , Vol. II, Sect. 667.
[E] *Year Books,* 21–22 Edward I (R.S.) , p. 436.

75. "The law hath yet another hold on you."

A cross action.

It frequently happens that a defendant to a bill in equity is advised to become himself a plaintiff in what is called a cross bill. He may require from the plaintiff in the original suit admissions of facts or the production of documents necessary for his defence. The original case may be founded on a deed or instrument which he may be entitled to have set aside for fraud or error; or he may on other grounds . . . be entitled not merely to resist the plaintiff's demand, but to have a decree giving him relief in respect of the property or transactions the subject of the original suit. He is not however able to obtain any such discovery or production of documents, or any such relief, without a cross bill.[A]

76. The evil of the Informer Clause in Statutes.

Shakespeare's inclusion of an obscure[B] statute which contained a provision that, as a penalty for its violation,

> The party 'gainst the which he doth contrive
> Shall seize one-half his goods. . . . [352]

is most interesting dramatically for obvious reasons.

Let us now see if the following quotation sheds any light on the lines quoted above in their relation to a most vexing and much discussed contemporary legal problem:

The number of statutes, old and new, in which the public at large was encouraged to enforce obedience to statutes by the promise of a share of the penalty imposed for disobedience was very large. A statute of 1488–1489 strongly approved this expedient; and as late as 1632 the Star Chamber, in order to suppress certain trade frauds, promised to give to informers half the fines which they imposed. But it was an expedient which was open to many obvious abuses. Old statutes which had been forgotten were unearthed and used as means to gratify ill-will. Litigation was stirred up simply in order that the informer might compound for a sum of money. Threats to sue were easy means of levying blackmail. A "turbidum genus" of informers arose whom Coke [in 1596] classes with "the monopolist, the concealer, and the dispencer with publick and profitable penal laws" as the four varieties of "viperous vermin," "which endeavoured to have eaten out the sides of church and commonwealth." Statutes of Elizabeth's reign attempted to cure the evil by small improvements in procedure. The informer was not allowed to sue by attorney, no compounding of the action was to be allowed without leave of the court, a year was fixed as the limitation for an informer's action unless the statute fixed a shorter period.[C]

Was Shakespeare's inclusion in the trial scene of a statute containing a public informer clause merely an ingenious device to heighten the dramatic suspense; or was it one more instance of his attempt, through the direct medium of the drama, to call attention to some of the obvious faults of the jurisprudence of his day?

The following is an example of the evil referred to above:

On Friday after the Octave of Hilary came William Gardener, gentleman, as well for the Queen as for himself, and produced a bill against Thomas Ducke in a plea that contrary to the statute of 12 January 5 Eliz. (1563) he had committed perjury, and was liable to a fine of £20, and if he had no goods to that value, he should be nailed by the ears to the pillory.[D]

[A] Holdsworth, *A History* . . . , VI. IX, p. 346, note 3.

[B] Keeton, *op. cit.,* p. 20. "There was also a similar law in England, as the audience . . . very well knew." Keeton does not cite the "similar law," and I have not been able to find it.

[C] Holdsworth, *A History* . . . , Vol. IV, pp. 356–357.

[D] Hotson, *op. cit.* p. 160.

77. "If it be proved against an alien. . . ."

When we consider that "The Jew was an alien both of church and state" and "also regarded as a species of *res nullius,*" the following official acts shed light on the subject of the citizenship of Jews in England from the time of William the Conqueror to the American Revolution:

In 1189 attacks were made on most of the Jewries in England, and their bonds were destroyed. ("Select Pleas etc., XVII, XVIII.")

In 1198 "Custodes Judaeorum" were appointed. ("Select Pleas etc., XX.")

A clause relating to usury upon debts owed to the Jews naturally found a place in the Magna Carta.

A severe ordinance was issued against them in 1253. ("Select Pleas etc., XXVIII, XXIX.")

In 1271 they were submitted to still further restrictions. ("McKechnie Magna Carta" 228.)

In 1275 usury was forbidden and they were required to wear a badge. ("3 Ed. I Statutes Rec. Com." i 221.)

In 1290 Edward I gained popularity, supplies and many escheats by banishing them. ("Select Pleas etc., XL.")

It was not until the Protectorate of Oliver Cromwell that they attempted to get permission to return. This permission was refused; but, after the Restoration, they began again to settle in England under the protection of the . . . king; and this exercise of praerogative was not called in question after the Revolution.[A]

Shylocke was, therefore, a product of a long tradition of bond litigation and usury practice. The sympathies of the Elizabethans were not with the Jew, and I have no doubt that the audiences took great delight in his defeat which, to them, was both justifiable and spectacular.

[A] Holdsworth, *A History* . . . , Vol. I, p. 46 *et seq.*

78. The attempts on Antonio's life.

The indirect attempt to seek the life of Antonio occurs in Act I, Scene iii, when Shylocke, feigning humility and good will, says:

> This kindness will I show.
> Go with me to a notary, seal me there
> Your single bond. . . . [146]

and the direct attempt takes place after the judgment when Shylocke, after whetting his knife in anticipation of the great moment of his vengeance, says:

> A sentence!
> Come, prepare! [304]

79. ". . . a Subject born."

The following is Justice Coke's summary of the English law regarding citizenship in 1609. This summary was the result of much litigation upon the subject, for Elizabethan England, with its vast expansion in trade and commerce, was confronted with the ever-increasing difficulties and complexities of diversity of citizenship:

There be regularly (unless it be in special Cases) three Incidents to a Subject born. 1. That the Parents be under the actual Obedience of the King. 2. That the Place of his Birth be within the King's Dominion, And 3. The Time of his Birth is chiefly to be considered, for he cannot be a Subject born of one Kingdom that was born under the ligeance of a King of another Kingdom, albeit afterwards one Kingdom descend to the King of the other.[B]

Once more the dramatist has followed contemporary English law very closely, for, by its strict terms, Shylocke was an "alien" and Antonio a "citizen."

[B] Coke, *Reports* . . . , Vol. VII, pp. 18a–18b.

80. ". . . multiplicity of suits."

The concurrence of jurisdiction may, in the greater number of cases in which it is exercised be justified by the propriety of preventing a multiplicity of suits.[A]

81 and 82. The jurisdiction of the Court of Chancery in regard to uses and trusts.

Holdsworth, in discussing the growth and development of the Chancellor's jurisdiction, duties, and powers in the sixteenth century says he had:

Firstly, the recognition, protection and development of uses and trusts. . . . Here it will be sufficient to say that the Chancellor so developed the duties of feoffees to uses, that is the persons to whom property had been conveyed on trust, that the interest of the cestui-que use, that is the person for whose benefit the property was conveyed, became a form of equitable ownership of a sort which has no parallel in any other system of law. This branch of equitable jurisdiction was from the first, and has always continued to be, its most important branch.[B]

This exclusive jurisdiction of the Court of Chancery was most lucrative and as Maitland has said: "In the early days of the court it made its fortune." The common law judges, ever jealous of the powers of the Chancellor, succeeded, therefore, in having the Statute of Uses (27 Henry VIII. c. 10) passed by Parliament in 1535. This statute did not abolish existing uses and trusts, nor did it prohibit the creation of new ones; nor deprive the Court of Chancery of its exclusive jurisdiction of all types of uses as shown by the following authority:

That statute adopted the plan of abolishing in certain cases the dual ownership of the feoffees to uses and the cestui-que use, by taking from the feoffees to uses so much of their legal estate as was sufficient to give to the cestui-que use a legal estate corresponding to his equitable interest. One result of the statute, therefore, was to give jurisdiction over the uses which had been thus turned into legal estates to the courts of common law. We shall see that for some time before 1535 the rivalry between the courts of common law and the court of Chancery had been growing acute; and, on that account, the common lawyers assisted the passage of a statute which gave them jurisdiction at the expense of the court of Chancery. But the statute did not apply to all uses. It did not, for instance, apply to cases where the feoffees were possessed of chattels real or personal to the use of others; nor did it apply to cases where they had active duties to perform, for instance if they were given land to the use that they should collect and pay the rents to a beneficiary. Thus the court of Chancery still retained some of its jurisdiction; and it regained much of the jurisdiction of which the statute had deprived it in the latter half of the seventeenth century.[C]

83. *Cestui que trust.*

Cestui que trust. He for whose benefit another person is seised of lands or tenements or is possessed of personal property.[D]

The phrase, *Cestui que trust,* is a barbarous Norman law French phrase; and is so ungainly and ill adapted to the English idiom, that it is surprising, that the good sense of the English legal profession has not long since banished it, and substituted some phrase in the English idiom, furnishing an analogous meaning. . . . But Beneficiary, though a little remote from the original meaning of the word, would be a very appropriate word, as it has not, as yet, acquired any general use in a different sense.[E]

[A] Fonblanque, *op. cit.*

[B] Holdsworth, *A History* . . . .Vol. I, p. 454.

[C] *Ibid.,* p. 455.

[D] Bouvier, *op. cit.,* Vol. I, p. 449.

[E] Joseph Story, *Commentaries on Equity Jurisprudence,* Vol. I, Ch. VII, p. 345, note 1.

84. The flexibility of equitable decrees.

The Chancellor was not bound by a particular form of judgment, as were the common law judges in actions of debt, detinue, trover, etc., but was free to enter any decree that he considered most apt to settle the difference between the parties, according to the dictates of "equity and good conscience." Thus, the standard by which the rights of the parties were adjudicated was flexible, as were the Chancellor's decrees which did not become absolute and final and could be altered upon the showing of good cause.[A]

85. "Contempt in case of disobedience."

This last official statement of the Chancellor shows, beyond a doubt, that Shakespeare knew the distinction between a decree *in personam* and a judgment *in rem*,[B] for Shylocke was permitted to leave the court without any formality other than the stern words of the Duke. This curt remark conveyed the following idea to Elizabethan audiences with tremendous dramatic effect: "Shylocke, you may leave the court but remember that you must obey the decree as entered in this cause or I shall declare you in contempt of this court and issue an attachment."[C]

86. *"The manner of entering decrees in times past."*

The following case illustrates the exact manner in which the decree in the case of Shylocke vs. Antonio might have been recorded in the perpetual records of English jurisprudence:

LINCOLN *v.* BEVORE.

The manner of entering decrees in times past.— A decree is made for the plaintant, as by the record thereof, signed with the Lord Chancellor's hand, plainly appeareth; and the said record is delivered to John Millicent, attorney for the plaintant, to be inrolled: . . . (Anno 5 & 6, Philip & Mary, fol. 15. [1558]) .[D]

87. "For half thy wealth, it is Antonio's. . . ."

The ultimate disposition of Shylocke's estate as decreed by the Lord Chancellor is shown in Table I, page 74.

88. Beneficiary.

A term suggested by Judge Story as a substitute for *cestui que trust,* and adopted to some extent.[E]

89. *"Trustee ordered to convey the lands according to the trust."*

The following case illustrates the power of the Chancellor to force the trustee to comply with the terms of the trust:

[A] See note 41.
[B] See note 41.
[C] See notes 67 and 68.

[D] *The English Reports*, Vol. 21, p. 18.
[E] Bouvier, *op. cit.,* Vol. I, p. 337.

YOUNG *v.* LEIGH.

Trustee ordered to convey the lands according to the trust.—The defendant by his answer confesseth he was joint-purchaser in trust with the plaintant's father, to them two, and to the heirs of the plaintant's father, of the lands in question; and that he never received any profits thereof; and that he meant at the plaintant's full age to convey the lands to the plaintant and his heirs, according to the trust; it is ordered and decreed, the defendant shall forthwith upon notice to him given, convey his estate in the land to the plaintant, and the heirs of his body begotten, with such remainder over, as in the last will and testament of the plaintant's father is expressed, at the costs of the plaintant: . . . (Anno 20 Eliz. [1577–78]) .[A]

90. "The other half comes to the general state. . . ."

Creation of the trust is traced in Table II. page 75

[A] *The English Reports,* Vol. 21, p. 36.

I

The result of the creation of a *use after a use.*[A]

	The one-half of Shylocke's estate to which Antonio was entitled.	
Legal[B] Title		Equitable[B] Title

Since the Equitable Title declared to Antonio necessitated no active duties, the Statute of Uses (1535) operated to bring the Legal Title over to the Equitable Title.[C]	The use declared to Antonio placed the Equitable Title in him.

↓ ↓

ANTONIO

First Use

Antonio had the Legal and Equitable Titles to this one-half of Shylocke's estate so long as Shylocke lived (*pur auter vie*).

During the life of Shylocke, Antonio was entitled to all of the income of the estate but not the principal. He had the power to manage and control the corpus of the estate but could not dissipate it and was held accountable for reasonable care in the management thereof.

There is a possible *gap,* or hiatus, in this use, for Antonio might die before Shylocke. If this occurred, the Equitable Estate would immediately go back to Shylocke and the Legal would follow it by the Statute of Uses. Then on the death of Shylocke, the Equitable Estate, in accordance with the terms of the declared use, would go to the named *cestui que use,* and the Legal Title would again follow by the Statute.

Legal Title — **Equitable Title**

The Statute of Uses applied here, for Lorenzo had no expressed duties to perform nor is there a use after his use. Therefore, by the Statute, the Legal Title followed the Equitable.	The declared use to become effective on the death of Shylocke placed the Equitable Title in Lorenzo.

↓ ↓

LORENZO

Use after the first *use*

1. By the terms of the use, Lorenzo held both the Legal and Equitable Title to this property, in fee, upon the decease of Shylocke.

2. The rule against perpetuities did not operate for the fee simple estate vested in Lorenzo on the death of Shylocke who was living when the use was declared.

3. Jessica had a dower right of one-third of this property but the right was extinguished upon her decease.

4. If Lorenzo left no will, the children of Lorenzo and Jessica took this estate by the law of descent and distribution, and, by the doctrine of *primo geniture* Shylocke's oldest grandson would receive all of the real property contained in this half of his estate.

5. Lorenzo, by will, had the power to dispose of his part of the estate in any manner he elected.

[A] The writer acknowledges his indebtedness to Professor William Arthur, School of Law, University of Colorado.

[B] The Chancellor, in accord with the fundamental principles of equity, always treated property, both personal and real, as though there were two separate estates or interests contained therein.

[C] In a *trust* there is some active duty for the trustee to perform and the Statute of Uses does not operate to join the Legal Title to the Equitable Title. In a *use* there is no duty for the holder of the Legal Title to perform, and the Statute *ipso facto* joins the two in the one holding the Equitable Title.

II
The result of the creation of the *Trust.*[A]

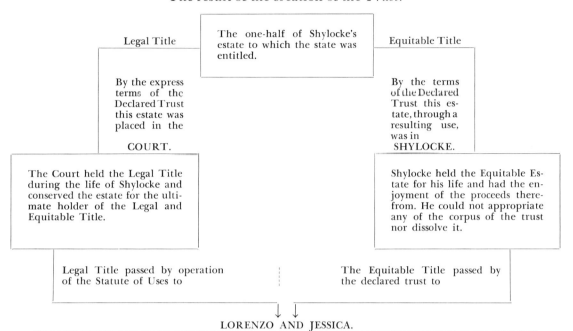

| Legal Title | The one-half of Shylocke's estate to which the state was entitled. | Equitable Title |

By the express terms of the Declared Trust this estate was placed in the

COURT.

By the terms of the Declared Trust this estate, through a resulting use, was in

SHYLOCKE.

The Court held the Legal Title during the life of Shylocke and conserved the estate for the ultimate holder of the Legal and Equitable Title.

Shylocke held the Equitable Estate for his life and had the enjoyment of the proceeds therefrom. He could not appropriate any of the corpus of the trust nor dissolve it.

Legal Title passed by operation of the Statute of Uses to

The Equitable Title passed by the declared trust to

↓ ↓

LORENZO AND JESSICA.

1. Lorenzo and Jessica were tenants by entirety of this estate and upon the death of either the survivor took the entire estate in fee.
2. The children of Jessica and Lorenzo took by will or the law of descent and distribution from the survivor.
3. If the survivor left no son and no will, the daughters took the estate as coparceners and could divide and partition it in any manner they elected.
4. If the survivor left a will, Shylocke's grandchildren took the estate according to the will.
5. Jessica had no right of dower to one-third of this estate.

Summary

1. Shylocke had the use and benefit of one-half of his estate until his death.
2. Antonio had the use and benefit of one-half of Shylocke's estate until Shylocke's death.
3. Upon the decease of Shylocke, Lorenzo received one-half of Shylocke's estate, in fee, and Jessica received one-third of this one-half as her dower right.
4. Upon the decease of Shylocke, Lorenzo and Jessica received the remaining one-half of Shylocke's estate, and the survivor took this entire one-half in fee.
5. Thus, during Shylocke's life he and Antonio were provided for and Lorenzo and Jessica received nothing until Shylocke's death.
6. If Jessica died first Lorenzo received all of each half of the estate.
7. If Lorenzo died first, Jessica received one-third of the first half of Shylocke's estate and all of the second half.
8. The children of Lorenzo and Jessica took each half of the estate by the law of descent and distribution or according to the terms of the will of the party devising his or her interest therein.

[A] The writer acknowledges his indebtedness to Professor William Arthur, School of Law, University of Colorado.

Conclusion

If the "strict court of Venice" had been the only tribunal before which the parties appeared, then by the justice of Shylocke's plea—unseasoned by mercy—there would have been the following inevitable results:

First: Shylocke would have cut the pound of flesh from off Antonio's breast which the law allowed.[A]

Second: Shylocke would not have been informed of any other hold which the law had upon him, or the consequences of his act, in relation to the statute referred to by Portia, for this would have raised more than one issue in a suit at common law.

Third: Shylocke would then have been tried in a criminal proceeding for his direct and indirect attempt against the life of a citizen, and, upon conviction, his life and half of his property would have been forfeit to the state.

Thus, at common law, Antonio would have lost his life and Shylocke both his life and that which was to him more dear, "the prop That doth sustain my house;" (375 et. seq.).

Through the use of equitable devices, Shakespeare obtained the following results:

First: He preserved the dramatic suspense so essential to the "bond plot."

Second: He spared the lives of Antonio and Shylocke.

Third: He provided for each of them during Shylocke's life and preserved the corpus of the estate for the ultimate use and benefit of Shylocke's heirs.

I hope that I have convinced my reader that it was the dramatist speaking in behalf of equity and not mere "words" when the Duke says: "Thou shalt see the difference of our spirits"; and that Shakespeare was issuing a mandatory injunction to all within his jurisdiction to see that the spirit of equity prevailed when the Duke, speaking not only to Shylocke but to all who have ears to hear, says:

"Get thee gone, but do it."

[A] White, *op. cit.*, p. 141. "It was axiomatic, at common law, that, where one held a legal right, he had all the remedies necessary to a full enjoyment of that right, for, otherwise, the right itself would be without avail."

Appendix I

"The number and variety of these injunctions . . . in this litigious age. . . ."

But it is obvious that these orders[A] would have been given no real relief if the parties could have continued to pursue their rights at law. Hence the ultimate resource of the Chancery, in a very large number of these cases, was the issue of an injunction against pursuing these legal proceedings, or, if judgment had been got, against enforcing the judgment. Thus injunctions were issued to stop abuses of process. In one case, the court stopped an action brought by A against a defendant merely to prevent him (the defendant) from giving evidence in another action brought by X against A; and in another it stopped an action brought with knowledge that the defendant's witnesses were all beyond the sea. On similar principles it issued injunctions to prevent the molestation of a tenant during an action on condition that he paid his rent into court, and to stay the execution of a hard judgment got against an executor de son tort till the case was heard by the court of Chancery. Injunctions both final and interlocutory to quiet possession were essential in order that the court might definitely settle questions of ownership, and enforce tenurial customs, agreements as to inclosure, and other similar agreements between a number of tenants in a manor or other district. Sometimes they were used to enforce a compromise between the parties to an action at law, or to prevent a plaintiff from vexing the defendant by simultaneous actions at common law and in equity. The number and variety of these injunctions show us that, in this litigious age, the power to issue them was the condition precedent for the exercise of this wide equitable jurisdiction to remedy the rigidity of the law.

The Evolution of the Character of Equity

We have seen that the theory underlying equitable interferences with the law made it necessary that equity should follow the law. The views of the mediaeval chancellors as to the relations between law and equity, and especially as to the extent to which equity ought to interfere with the law, had been ably summarized by St. Germain; and these views, as thus summarized, were acted upon all through this period. But it is equally clear,

---

[A] See note 67 which refers to this passage.

that, in the absence of any fixed principles to guide the chancellor as to what course was in the circumstances equitable, the question whether in any given case relief should be granted, depended upon the view which the chancellor took of the facts of the case. The court of Chancery was a court of conscience; and the chancellor decreed for the plaintiff or the defendant as his conscience dictated.

The entire dependence of the principles of equity upon the conscience of one man was a useful weapon to the common lawyers. "For some men think," wrote the Serjeant, "that if they tread upon two straws that lie across they offend in conscience, and some man thinketh that if he lack money, and another hath too much, that he may take part of his with conscience; and so divers men, divers conscience." Norburie, writing soon after the fall of Bacon, said that, "the boundless power of the Chancery in not having rules and grounds written and prescribed unto it, in what cases it shall give relief and what not, is the cause of much discontent and distraction to the King's subjects, and clamours against the Lord Chancellor." Selden's well-known jest upon the variations of equity is another instance of the same sort of criticism.

It is clear from Lambard that, at the close of the sixteenth century, the resulting uncertainty of the rules of equity was leading men to consider whether it was not possible to lay down some certain rules for the administration of equity, without destroying entirely that discretionary character of the relief given, which was its very essence. He offers no solution of this problem. But, while he was writing, two sets of circumstances were beginning to modify the character of equity; and it is through this modification that the solution was destined eventually to come. Firstly, the political reasons which were tending to differentiate the jurisdiction of the chancellor from that of the Council, the Star Chamber, the court of Admiralty, and the ecclesiastical courts, and to settle the relations between the common law courts and the court of Chancery, were helping to settle the sphere of the court's jurisdiction. Secondly, the growth of the practice of citing cases as precedents was an influence which was helping, not only to settle still more exactly the sphere of the court's jurisdiction, but also to make some fixed rules for the exercise of the chancellor's discretion. But though, during this period, these two sets of circumstances were fast settling the sphere of the chancellor's jurisdiction, comparatively little progress had as yet been made in the fettering of his discretion in matters which fell within his jurisdiction. The chancellors still considered themselves very free to act whenever they thought that they could secure substantial justice by their action. In the *Earl of Oxford's* Case, for instance, equity interfered with the operation of a statute in a manner which would have been impossible at a later period. In fact, during the whole of this period and later, the court of Chancery was actually, and not merely technically, a court of conscience. For this reason the contents of the rules of equity, and therefore the relation of equity to the law, continued to depend to a considerable extent upon the conscience of the chancellor. We can only see the remote beginnings of the causes which will, by settling the contents of these rules, make the court only technically a court of conscience; and, in these last days, enable a judge of the Chancery Division of the High Court to deny that it is in any sense a court of this character.[A]

[A] Holdsworth, *A History* . . . , Vol. V, pp. 335–338.

Appendix II

UNIVERSITY OF COLORADO
SCHOOL OF LAW
BOULDER, COLORADO

Mr. Mark Edwin Andrews
8 Shadder Way
Houston, Texas
April 23, 1964

Dear Mr. Andrews:

Our library has recently prepared an exhibit entitled "Shakespeare
and the Law." In searching for materials for this exhibit, we came across
an unbound manuscript called *Law vs. Equity in "The Merchant of
Venice."* It was written at the University of Colorado in 1935 by one
Mark Edwin Andrews. The author acknowledges the help he received from
the University of Colorado Law Library in the preface.

We have had the manuscript bound, and it is the focal point of the
exhibit. I am writing to find out if you are the author of the manuscript.
If so, I would like to commend you for a fine, scholarly work.

If this book has never been published, I would like to strongly recom-
mend that you consider having it published. I feel that it makes a significant contribution to the subject of Shakespeare.

I am looking forward to hearing from you.

Sincerely,

Roy M. Mersky
Professor of Law and
Law Librarian

MARK EDWIN ANDREWS
BANK OF THE SOUTHWEST BUILDING
HOUSTON, TEXAS 77002

Professor Roy M. Mersky
Fleming Law Building
Boulder, Colorado 80304   April 27, 1964

Dear Professor Mersky:

You are correct in your assumption. I am the one who wrote the manuscript; and your letter has brought back many happy memories of the summers which we spent in Boulder.

For several years we leased the home of Dean Bushee which is adjacent to Dean Durham's home. I busied myself by taking courses in law, economics and English literature. I had the rare opportunity to take courses from "Pop" Arthur, Professor Wyhoffen, Dean Stearns, Dean Clark of Yale, Dean Rutledge of Iowa, Dean Gavit of Indiana and many others.

One summer Dr. Spaeth who had taught me Shakespeare at Princeton was there; and so was Dr. Hudson who was Chairman of the English Department at Princeton. I took their courses at Boulder again and one was Dr. Spaeth's Shakespeare course.

One day we were studying "The Merchant of Venice" and Dr. Spaeth read the "Quality of Mercy" speech. He then asked me what I thought of it as a legal argument. I replied that I thought it was more of an equitable plea than a legal argument. Dr. Spaeth did not reply; but, as soon as class was over, he grabbed my arm and said: "Ed, what did you mean by your reply about a legal argument and an equitable plea?"

Dr. Spaeth always had luncheon with us when he lectured; and, on our way home, I told him I wanted to go by the Guggenheim Library to find out when the case of Glanville versus Courtney was decided. I told him that this case settled the 300 year old conflict between law and equity in English jurisprudence; and maybe Shakespeare was dramatizing this struggle. We found that Glanville versus Courtney was decided in 1616 by a special commission appointed by King James. At luncheon we went over the trial scene and I showed him some of the legal and equitable points raised in it. I was surprised to discover the sharp break between the use of legal terms and devices in the first 304 lines of the scene and equitable terms and procedure in the last 100 lines. This excited Dr. Spaeth very much and he asked me to do a paper for the class and have it finished in two weeks.

I started working, that June day, in the library; and I realized at once that my assumption was correct. There it was—The trial in the court of law, beginning with "Is Antonio here", and ending with a judgment *in rem,* "A pound of that same merchant's flesh is thine: The court awards it and the law doth give it" (line 300).

Then Portia says: "Tarry a little; there is something else" (line 305) and then all of the powers of Equity are brought into play. The hearing for the injunction in the court of Chancery ends with the Chancellor's decree, *in personam,* to Shylock. "Get thee gone but do it".

I did not finish the "two week" paper until September because the more research I did, and the more books I turned o'er (line 156), the more "authorities", "precedents", "statutes", "opinions", and "decrees" I found to prove that Shakespeare *was* dramatizing this great conflict.

When I finished the manuscript I sent copies to Dr. Spaeth, Justice Rutledge and Justice Stone who wrote the introduction. All of them thought I should publish the manuscript and Dr. Spaeth and Dr. Hudson were very insistent about it. At the time I decided not to publish the manuscript because I did not have the time to put it into final form. It was all done in about three months and I wanted to "tighten it up" here and there. I also wanted to make it more easily readable. They insisted that it was a piece of scholarship which shed an entirely new light on the trial scene and proved, beyond doubt, that Shakespeare was aware of this struggle as were his contemporaries, Lord Chief Justice Coke, Lord Chancellor Ellesmere, and Sir Francis Bacon; and that the play must have influenced the final outcome of the conflict between Law and Equity in English jurisprudence.

I do appreciate your letter very much and I am grateful for the wonderful library at Boulder which made the work possible.

It is most gratifying to have you say the work is worthy of publication and to know that you deem it of sufficient merit to have had it bound and made a part of the Shakespeare exhibit at the law library.

I would like very much to have the work published; and I would appreciate any suggestions you may have as to any rearrangement of the material and a possible publisher. I would also like to know if there would be a market at all for such a book.

It has been almost thirty years since I did the work; and I have enjoyed reading over a copy of the manuscript this last week end.

Again thank you for your kindness and your interest in this manuscript "yellowed with age".

Yours sincerely,
Mark Edwin Andrews

Bibliography

AMES, J. B. *Selection of Cases in Equity Jurisdiction,* Vol. I. Cambridge: Harvard University Press, 1904.

BACON, SIR FRANCIS. *Law Tracts.* London: F. and R. Nutt, 1737.

———. *The Reading upon The Statutes of Uses.* London: W. Stratford, 1804.

BARBOUR, ———. *History of Contracts in Early English Equity,* Four Oxford Studies.

BEAWES, WYNDHAM. *Lex Mercatoria Rediviva: or, a complete Code of Commercial Law, being a General Guide to all Men in Business,* 5th ed. London: R. Baldwin, T. Longman, 1792.

BIRCH, THOMAS. *Memoirs of the Reign of Queen Elizabeth.* London: A. Millar, 1754.

BIRKENHEAD, THE EARL OF. *Fourteen English Judges.* London: Cassell and Company, Ltd., 1926.

BISPHAM, G. T. *The Principles of Equity,* 9th ed. New York: The Banks Law Publishing Co., 1915.

BLACKSTONE, SIR WILLIAM. *Tracts chiefly relating to the Antiquities and Laws of England.* Oxford: The Clarendon Press, 1771.

———. *Commentaries on the Laws of England,* 4 vols. Philadelphia: Rees Welsh & Co., 1900.

BOLLES, FRANK. *Important English Statutes,* 3rd ed. Cambridge: Waterman and Amee, 1888.

BOUVIER, JOHN. *Law Dictionary,* 8th ed., Vols. I, II, III. Kansas City, Missouri: Vernon Law Book Company, 1914.

BRACTON, HENRY DE. *De Legibus et Consuetudinibus Angliae.* London: Flesher & Young, 1640.

———. *Notebook,* 3 vols. London: 1887.

BROOM, HERBERT. *Legal Maxims,* 7th ed. Philadelphia: T. & J. W. Johnson & Co., 1874.

CAMPBELL, JOHN LORD. *Lives of the Lord Chancellors,* Vol. II. Boston: Estes & Lauriat, 1874.

———. *Shakespeare's Legal Acquirements.* London: John Murray, 1859.

Cases in the High Court of Chancery. London: John Walthoe, 1707.

CHRISTIAN, CHITTY, LEE, HOVENDEN, AND RYLAND. *Commentaries on the Laws of England, by Sir William Blackstone, Knt.,* Vols. I, II. Philadelphia: J. B. Lippincott & Co., 1858.

COKE, SIR EDWARD. *Institutes of the Laws of England; or, a Commentary upon Littleton: Not the Name of the Author only, but of the Law Itself,* 15th ed., Vols. I, II, III. London: E. and R. Brooke, 1744, 1797; E. and R. Nutt and R. Gosling, 1738.

———. *The Reports of Sir Edward Coke, Knt. In English, In thirteen Parts Compleat,* Parts I–XIII. London: E. and R. Nutt, 1738.

———. *Three Law Tracts.* London: J. Worrall, 1764.

———. *Chronica Juridicialia,* 3rd ed. London: D. Browne, 1739.

Corpus Juris, 72 vols. New York: The American Law Book Company, 1914–1937.

DUGDALE, SIR WILLIAM. *Origines Juridiciales; or, Historical Memorials of English Laws, Courts of Justice,* 3rd ed. London: Christop, Wilkinson, Tho. Dring, and Charles Harper, 1680.

The English Reports, Full Reprint, Vols. 1–176. Edinburgh: William Green & Sons, 1900.

FITZ-HERBERT, SIR ANTHONY. *Natura Brevium,* 9th ed. Dublin: H. Watts, 1793.

FONBLANQUE, JOHN W. M. *Equity,* 10th ed. London: 1852.

FREEMAN, A. C. *A Treatise of the Law of Judgments,* 4th ed., Vol. I. San Francisco: Bancroft-Whitney Company, 1892.

GILBERT, SIR GEOFFREY. *A Treatise on the Court of Exchequer.* London: E. and R. Nutt, 1758.

——. *The Law of Uses and Trusts,* 3rd ed. London: W. Reed, 1811.

HARGRAVE, FRANCIS. *Collection of Tracts Relative to the Law of England,* 2 vols. London: Wright, 1787.

HOLDSWORTH, SIR WILLIAM S. *A History of English Law,* 3rd ed., Vols. 1–9. Boston: Little, Brown, and Company, 1922.

——. *Sources and Literature of English Law.* Oxford: The Clarendon Press, 1925.

HOLMES, OLIVER WENDELL. *The Common Law.* Boston: Little, Brown, and Company, 1881.

HOTSON, LESLIE. *Shakespeare versus Shallow.* Boston: Little, Brown, and Company, 1931.

JENKS, EDWARD. *Short History of English Law,* 2nd ed. Boston: Little, Brown, and Company, 1922.

KEETON, G. W. *Shakespeare and His Legal Problems.* London: A. & C. Black, 1930.

MORGAN, E. M. *Introduction to the Study of Law.* Chicago: Callaghan and Company, 1926.

MURRAY, SIR JAMES. *New English Dictionary.* Oxford: The Clarendon Press, 1933.

PLOWDEN, EDMUND. *The Commentaries, or Reports . . . ,* Parts I, II. London: Edward Brooke, 1779.

POLLOCK, SIR FREDERICK and FREDERIC WILLIAM MAITLAND. *The History of English Law,* Vols. I, II. Cambridge: The University Press, 1911.

POMEROY, J. N. *A Treatise on Equity Jurisprudence,* student's ed. San Francisco: Bancroft-Whitney Company, 1907.

POTTON, E. *Tables and Index to A History of English Law by Sir William Holdsworth.* London: Methuen & Co., Ltd., 1932.

Registrum Brevium Tam Originalium, Quam Judicialium, 4th ed. London: Thomas Bassett, 1687.

ROLLE, SIR HENRY. *Un Abridgment des Plusieurs Cases et Resolutions del Common Ley.* London: A. Crooke, W. Leake, A. Roper, 1688.

SELDEN, JOHN. *Ad fletam dissertatio, "Fleta."* London: 1647.

——. *Joannis Sel Deni Jurisconsulti Opera Omnia,* Vols. I, II, III. London: J. Walthoe, G. Conyers, 1726.

——. *Table Talk.* Edited by Sir Frederick Pollock. London: Quaritch, 1927.

SHARSWOOD, GEORGE. *Commentaries by Sir William Blackstone, Knt.,* Vols. I, II. Philadelphia: J. B. Lippincott & Co., 1874.

STORY, JOSEPH. *Commentaries on Equity Jurisprudence,* 5th ed., Vols. I, II. London: Little, Brown, and Company, 1849.

STYLE, WILLIAM. *Narrationes Modernae, Or Modern Reports Begun in the now Upper Bench Court at Westminster.* London: W. Lee, D. Pakeman, G. Bedel, and C. Adams, 1658.

TURNER, R. W. *The Equity of Redemption.* Cambridge: The University Press, 1931.

WALSH, W. F. *A Treatise on Equity.* Chicago: Callaghan and Company, 1930.

——. *A Treatise on Mortgages.* Chicago: Callaghan and Company, 1934.

WHITE, E. J. *Commentaries on the Law in Shakespeare,* 2nd ed. St. Louis: Thomas Law Book Company.

WIGMORE, J. H. *A Treatise on . . . Evidence,* 2nd ed., Vols. 1–5. Boston: Little, Brown, and Company, 1923.

——. *Evidence in Trials at Common Law,* Vols. I, II. Boston: Little, Brown and Company, 1904.

Year Books, or Les Reports Des Cases Argue & Adjudge in le Temps del' Roy. 21, 22, 30 Edward I; 1–19 Edward II; 1–10, 17–39, 40–50 Edward III; 1–14 Henry IV; 1–19 Henry V; 1–39 Henry VI; 9, 22 Edward IV; Edward V; 4–7 Richard III; Henry VII; Henry VIII.

And many an error by the same example,
Will rush into the state: It cannot be.

Iew. A *Daniel* come to iudgement, yea a *Daniel*.
O wise young Iudge, how do I honour thee.

Por. I pray you let me looke vpon the bond.

Iew. Heere 'tis most reuerend Doctor, heere it is.

Por. *Shylocke*, there's thrice thy monie offered thee.

Shy. An oath, an oath, I haue an oath in heauen:
Shall I lay periurie vpon my soule?
No not for Venice.

Por. Why this bond is forfeit,
And lawfully by this the Iew may claime
A pound of flesh, to be by him cut off
Neerest the Merchants heart; be mercifull,
Take thrice thy money, bid me teare the bond.

Iew. When it is paid according to the tenure.
It doth appeare you are a worthy Iudge:
you know the Law, your exposition
Hath beene most sound. I charge you by the Law,
Whereof you are a well-deseruing pillar,
Proceede to iudgement: By my soule I sweare,
There is no power in the tongue of man
To alter me: I stay heere on my bond.

An. Most heartily I do beseech the Court
To giue the iudgement.

Por. Why then thus it is:
you must prepare your bosome for his knife.

Iew. O noble Iudge, O excellent yong man.

Por. For the intent and purpose of the Law
Hath full relation to the penaltie,
Which heere appeareth due vpon the bond.

Iew. 'Tis verie true: O wise and vpright Iudge,
How much more elder art thou then thy lookes?

Por. Therefore lay bare your bosome.

Iew. I, his brest,
So sayes the bond, doth it not noble Iudge?
Neerest his heart, those are the very words.

Por. It is so: Are there ballance heere to weigh the
flesh?

Iew. I haue them ready.

Por. Haue by some Surgeon *Shylock* on your charge
To stop his wounds, least he should bleede to death.

Iew. It is not nominated in the bond?

Por. It is not so exprest: but what of that?
'Twere good you do so much for charitie.

Iew. I cannot finde it, 'tis not in the bond.

Por. Come Merchant, haue you any thing to say?

Ant. But little: I am arm'd and well prepar'd.
Giue me your hand *Bassanio*, fare you well,
Greeue not that I am falne to this for you:
For heerein fortune shewes her selfe more kinde
Then is her custome. It is still her vse,
To let the wretched man out-liue his wealth,
To view with hollow eye, and wrinkled brow
An age of pouerty. From which lingring penance
Of such miserie, doth she cut me off:
Commend me to your honourable Wife,
Tell her the processe of *Anthonio's* end
Say how I lou'd you; speake me faire in death:
And when the tale is told, bid her be iudge,
Whether *Bassanio* had not once a Loue:
Repent not you that you shall loose your friend,
And he repents not that he payes your debt.
For if the Iew do cut but deepe enough,
Ile pay it instantly, with all my heart.

Bass. Anthonio, I am married to a wife,

Which is as deere to me as life it selfe,
But life it selfe, my wife, and all the world,
Are not with me esteem'd aboue thy life.
I would loose all, I sacrifice them all
Heere to this deuill, to deliuer you.

Por. Your wife would giue you little thanks for that
If she were by to heare you make the offer.

Gra. I haue a wife whom I protest I loue,
I would she were in heauen, so she could
Intreat some power to change this currish Iew.

Ner. 'Tis well you offer it behinde her backe,
The wish would make else an vnquiet house. (ter

Iew. These be the Christian husbands: I haue a daugh-
Would any of the stocke of *Barrabas*
Had beene her husband, rather then a Christian.
We trifle time, I pray thee pursue sentence.

Por. A pound of that same marchants flesh is thine,
The Court awards it, and the law doth giue it.

Iew. Most rightfull Iudge.

Por. And you must cut this flesh from off his breast,
The Law allowes it, and the Court awards it.

Iew. Most learned Iudge, a sentence, come prepare.

Por. Tarry a little, there is something else,
This bond doth giue thee heere no iot of bloud,
The words expresly are a pound of flesh:
Then take thy bond, take thou thy pound of flesh,
But in the cutting it, if thou dost shed
One drop of Christian bloud, thy lands and goods
Are by the Lawes of Venice confiscate
Vnto the state of Venice.

Gra. O vpright Iudge,
Marke Iew, ô learned Iudge.

Shy. Is that the law?

Por. Thy selfe shalt see the Act:
For as thou vrgest iustice, be assur'd
Thou shalt haue iustice more then thou desirest.

Gra. O learned Iudge, mark Iew, a learned Iudge.

Iew. I take this offer then, pay the bond thrice,
And let the Christian goe.

Bass. Heere is the money.

Por. Soft, the Iew shall haue all iustice, soft, no haste,
He shall haue nothing but the penalty.

Gra. O Iew, an vpright Iudge, a learned Iudge.

Por. Therefore prepare thee to cut off the flesh,
Shed thou no bloud, nor cut thou lesse nor more
But iust a pound of flesh: if thou tak'st more
Or lesse then a iust pound, be it so much
As makes it light or heauy in the substance,
Or the deuision of the twentieth part
Of one poore scruple, nay if the scale doe turne
But in the estimation of a hayre,
Thou diest, and all thy goods are confiscate.

Gra. A second *Daniel*, a *Daniel* Iew,
Now infidell I haue thee on the hip.

Por. Why doth the Iew pause, take thy forfeiture.

Shy. Giue me my principall, and let me goe.

Bass. I haue it ready for thee, heere it is.

Por. He hath refus'd it in the open Court,
He shall haue meerly iustice and his bond.

Gra. A *Daniel* still say I, a second *Daniel*,
I thanke thee Iew for teaching me that word.

Shy. Shall I not haue barely my principall?

Por. Thou shalt haue nothing but the forfeiture,
To be taken so at thy perill Iew.

Shy. Why then the Deuill giue him good of it:
Ile stay no longer question.

Por. Tarry